# MICHAEL SMITH'S
## N·E·W
# ENGLISH
## COOKERY

# *M*ICHAEL *S*MITH'S
# *E* NGLISH
## N•E•W
## COOKERY

*B*RITISH *B*ROADCASTING *C*ORPORATION

Book design: Glyn Davies
Photographs: Jem Grischotti
Illustrations: Robert Kettle


*Cover photo shows:*
Breasts of Chicken with Pecans and Apples and Stilton Sauce
Lemon Ice (front); Pan-fried Fillet Steak with Mustard and Caper Sauce
Cream of Mussel Soup with Saffron (back)


The BBC would like to thank Harvey Nichols
and Rosenthal for providing some of the dishes
used in the photographs.

First published 1985

Published by the British Broadcasting Corporation
35 Marylebone High Street, London W1M 4AA

Typeset in 12/13 Caslon Old Face by Phoenix Photosetting, Chatham
Printed and bound by Mackays of Chatham Limited
Colour origination by Bridge Graphics Limited, Hull
Colour printed by Chorley and Pickersgill Limited, Leeds


ISBN 0 563 20403 6 (paperback)
0 563 20443 5 (hardback)

*'I reserve the right to change my ideas
in the light of new experiences in life.'*

MICHAEL SMITH

Sheila Thorne  June 1986

# CONTENTS

◆

INTRODUCTION *9*

SOUPS *19*

STARTERS *43*

SALADS *63*

VEGETABLES *83*

FISH *93*

POULTRY AND GAME *111*

MEAT *141*

COLD PUDDINGS AND ICES *167*

HOT PUDDINGS *199*

INDEX *219*

# CONVERSION TABLES

◆

*A*LL these are *approximate* conversions, which have either been rounded up or down. In a few recipes it has been necessary to modify them very slightly. Never mix metric and imperial measures in one recipe; stick to one system or the other.

| Weights | |
|---|---|
| ½ oz | 10 g |
| 1 | 25 |
| 1½ | 40 |
| 2 | 50 |
| 3 | 75 |
| 4 | 110 |
| 5 | 150 |
| 6 | 175 |
| 7 | 200 |
| 8 | 225 |
| 9 | 250 |
| 10 | 275 |
| 12 | 350 |
| 13 | 375 |
| 14 | 400 |
| 15 | 425 |
| 1 lb | 450 |
| 1¼ | 550 |
| 1½ | 700 |
| 2 | 900 |
| 3 | 1.4 kg |
| 4 | 1.8 |
| 5 | 2.3 |

| Volume | |
|---|---|
| 1 fl oz | 25 ml |
| 2 | 50 |
| 3 | 75 |
| 5 (¼ pint) | 150 |
| 10 (½) | 275 |
| 15 (¾) | 400 |
| 1 pint | 570 |
| 1¼ | 700 |
| 1½ | 900 |
| 1¾ | 1 litre |
| 2 | 1.1 |
| 2¼ | 1.3 |
| 2½ | 1.4 |
| 2¾ | 1.6 |
| 3 | 1.75 |
| 3¼ | 1.8 |
| 3½ | 2 |
| 3¾ | 2.1 |
| 4 | 2.3 |
| 5 | 2.8 |
| 6 | 3.4 |
| 7 | 4.0 |
| 8 (1 gal) | 4.5 |

| Measurements | |
|---|---|
| ¼ inch | 0.5 cm |
| ½ | 1 |
| 1 | 2.5 |
| 2 | 5 |
| 3 | 7.5 |
| 4 | 10 |
| 6 | 15 |
| 7 | 18 |
| 8 | 20.5 |
| 9 | 23 |
| 11 | 28 |
| 12 | 30.5 |

| Oven temperatures | | |
|---|---|---|
| Mark 1 | 275°F | 140°C |
| 2 | 300 | 150 |
| 3 | 325 | 170 |
| 4 | 350 | 180 |
| 5 | 375 | 190 |
| 6 | 400 | 200 |
| 7 | 425 | 220 |
| 8 | 450 | 230 |
| 9 | 475 | 240 |

# *I*NTRODUCTION

◆

W<sub>E</sub> British have at least three major assets – our individuality, our eccentricity, and our total freedom of expression. These, together with our gigantic inventiveness in the eighteenth and nineteenth centuries in the field of industry and overseas expansion, led us to greatness. We also have an amazing capacity for tolerance: our police are still unarmed, our people are still free to stand on their hind legs and hold forth on any subject, political or otherwise, without fear of being locked away: Speakers' Corner alone is evidence of this great liberty; Parliament, and the democratic paths to it, another. It could be said, and by many *is* said, that tolerance is the near neighbour of apathy and perhaps weakness; but surely that happens when we tolerate other people's fallibilities and irresponsibilities, but not their 'creativeness', proclivities or political leanings. Again, eccentricity can be seen as perverseness – and when it comes to our attitude to food we *are* perverse.

Tourism today is coming close to being our second major export industry. Some 14 million visitors come to Britain every year – a figure which must be maintained and increased: these tourists place over £5½ *billion* into our national coffers. On the whole we look after our tourists well, though there are those who would deny them this service, and this is where we are perverse. We welcome and need their money, yet we resent their presence, their languages and accents, particularly in the streets and shops of our tourist towns and villages. Above all, we resent the effort entailed in providing them with decent food.

The average visitor from abroad can get American food (the burger), Italian (pizza '*e*' pasta), Greek (moussaka and taramasalata), Chinese (sweet and sour), Japanese (sushi and tempura), German and Austrian (schnitzels and the now ubiquitous Black Forest gâteau), and French (the even more ubiquitous quiches and pâtés based on emulsified fats as the contents of those country pottery bowls clearly shows). And I haven't even mentioned India, with its tandooris and abundant same-tasting curries, or the Danish, Thai, Indonesian, Turkish, Armenian, Jewish, Arab and Mexican restaurants, each contributing their particular national dishes to our chequerboard.

There is rightly a place for any or all of these, not only to supply the individual ethnic groups living here (and I'm delighted you can now get soul food in London *and* Birmingham), but for us to have the opportunity to taste the food of another culture. But this should not be at the expense of our *own*.

A 'Taste of Britain' promotion, started by the English Tourist Board in 1975, was abandoned in 1983 because of the lack of funds! Can you imagine that? Yet it is a fact. If you are a tourist coming to Britain for the first time, surely you should expect to encounter British food at its best, yet in the greatest capital city in the world you will be hard put to count on your ten fingers anywhere offering an across-the-board selection of our national dishes. And where among the thousands of restaurants in this city of over 12 million people is there one serving Scottish, Irish or Welsh food?

There are reasons for all this. One is that the traditional English bill of fare, which required that guests sat at the table at a fixed time to enjoy a succulent plateful cut from one of our renowned roast joints, followed by pudding, no longer fits in to our rushed style of twentieth-century living (although the appearance of carveries perhaps heralds the rebirth of this habit). But perhaps the most important reason is our inherent guilt complex about food. Two world wars, recessions and unemployment, and even the public school system (where headmasters 'bled-off' money meant for feeding their charges into their own pockets) have resulted over the years in the debasement of our national dishes. Where carbohydrate bulk is a welcome foundation for the rugby field, and cheap, sweet stodgy puddings are seen as a Sunday treat, the bland, if not inedible, food that ensues soon breeds a race of men and women who are completely inured to encountering nothing of interest on their plates.

Religion, too, has a lot to answer for. Oh yes, this hot potato cannot be dismissed, for the Puritans rid us of our spices, the Methodists of our liquor, and now other modern cults are attempting to rid us of our meat, fish and poultry, as they head down what is for me the wrong dietary path. I'm a 'moderation-in-all-things' and 'a-little-bit-of-what-you-fancy' man.

In 1972 Faber and Faber published my book *Fine English Cookery*. This was the culmination of twenty years' effort to restore and improve those recipes I considered should still be seen on our tables. I was not alone, though others of a similar mind then were few, and for the record I would like to mention some of them: the late Constance Spry, and Rosemary Hume of *Cordon Bleu* fame, Sheila Hutchins, Frances Coulson and Brian Sack of Sharrow Bay, and George Perry Smith of The Hole-in-the-Wall in Bath. (In recent years, of course, we have been joined by Jane Grigson, that most literate of writers on food.) We were all considered eccentric, we were laughed at, albeit kindly, and people saw it as a 'let's dress up' and try a bit of

Olde Englande. Happily, there were some who enjoyed and accepted, and certainly understood, what we were aiming at.

It is fashion perhaps that urges all cooks and cookery writers to do something new and different. The *cuisine minceur* that Michel Guérard devised was certainly a move towards the current trend for healthier eating (although many felt it was a fad, emanating from the medics of the United States, cleverly exploited by the French). Hot on its trail came *nouvelle cuisine*, enlarging on (and often disagreeing with) Guérard's preaching. This 'small-is-beautiful' approach is safe in the hands of its inventors, Paul Bocuse, Roger Vergé and their followers, and of its principal introducers to this country, Michel and Albert Roux and Anton Mosiman, but is about as unsafe as any art is if left in the hands of the inexperienced, incapable, or uncreative. *Nouvelle cuisine* may be something new to write about, but the magical mosaics it demands are beyond the capabilities of most, and the fine balancing of colour, texture and taste requires a true artist. Many of the combinations I have found presented in the name of *nouvelle cuisine* seem to me pretty unacceptable, yet many self-styled food critics have hailed the appearance of this new way of cooking (and eating) as something they are bound to comment on, offering criticisms they are ill-equipped to pen.

This could never happen in the field of music or literature where the critic is educated to a high level in his art. Can you imagine a critic putting pen to paper on the subject of a new symphony by Menotti, Tippett or Boulez without a profound knowledge of his subject? In the field of food I have seen articles by cub-journalists slating the craft of such eminent chefs as Malcolm Reid, Kenneth Bell, Nico Ladenis, not to speak of myself. The French, however, in spite of putting the amateur cook back in the kitchen, ne'er to enjoy a 'G. and T.' in comfort again, lest the mind becomes too blurred to create the mosaics of pattern expected of them, have given some of us the jolt necessary to look again at English food and give it a push into the future, without losing its identity and without making it unacceptably exclusive. This is what *New English Cookery* is all about.

$M$ICHAEL SMITH
*London, 1985*

$A$ FEW notes about some basic ingredients:

## BUTTER

I am often asked why I demand unsalted butter in recipes. The answers are simple: good butter gives an excellent flavour unsurpassed by any other cooking medium; unsalted butter is essential for cakes, puddings, buttercreams and so on; you can always add salt; there is less water and less sediment in unsalted butters.

## MARGARINE

The arguments for and against using margarines are complex. Many cheaper brands are made from refined whale or fish oils, a fact not generally known to the public. I advocate using good butter for cooking as it is a natural product and there is no flavour like it. In my 'moderation-in-all-things' approach, though, I suggest that you cut down your butter intake by *never* having it on toast or bread, or with cheese and biscuits.

## CREAMS

The consistency and quality of creams vary throughout the country, from the rich, thick double cream of single-herd farms to the thin, almost grey single cream found in the cheaper supermarkets. This is going to affect the consistency and taste of your dish, but the choice has to be yours, selecting the best available in your particular area.

Whilst my reputation as a 'cream-with-everything man' is probably justified, I do try to keep things in perspective. A quarter of a pint (150 ml) of cream added to a dish for four to six people can hardly be said to be lavish.

## OILS

There is a great variety of oils available in the shops for use in salad dressings and for cooking. I suggest you use olive oil, or a mixture of olive and nut oil or soy oil. The last is almost flavourless and is excellent for frying.

I find the flavour of corn, rape-seed, maize and other cheap oils totally unacceptable in cooking, and I never use them.

For salads, I ring the changes by using walnut, hazelnut, grape-seed and almond oils. However, oils do deteriorate quite quickly and should be bought in smallish quantities, depending on how regularly you use them: do not keep them for more than two to three months after purchase (less in the summer).

Oil used in a deep fryer should be *strained after each use* and stored in a dark place in an airtight plastic container. It should also be changed frequently as overheating and oversaturating cause decomposition. Soy is the best for frying.

## SUGARS

Natural refined sugars such as muscovado, Barbados and demerara sugars can be substituted in most recipes where white sugar is called for. However, these sugars have very pronounced rich flavours and will change the taste of a dish, which is not always desirable. For example, dark sugar in coffee changes the flavour of the coffee totally. But in recipes using chocolate, or in spicy dishes, some salad dressings and preserves, dark sugars can add a desirable extra tone to the overall flavour which white sugar cannot. They marry well with dates, prunes, figs, mangoes, even rhubarb, and sometimes with oranges and apricots. However, I would never use these rich-toned sugars with any fresh-flavoured English berries, fresh currants or with apples, pears and lemons, grapefruit or grapes (an unrefined light cane sugar, though, is acceptable as it will not mar the clean flavour of these fruits).

Icing sugar looks better than caster sugar for dredging cakes, biscuits and puddings.

## HONEYS

When honey is called for I suggest you use one or other of the natural flower or heather honeys. There are cheaper brands of honey available, but these are too strong, being made by bees that are fed on beet sugar syrup, and to me their flavour is intrusive and caramelly. In fact, I find that heather honey is too powerful for many delicate sauces (it's ideal for spreading on crumpets, though!) and for most cooking purposes I recommend lime or orange-blossom honey.

## FLOUR

Health-food flours or whole grain or whole wheat flours are necessary for a good daily diet. I restrict them, though, to bread-making – I consider fine white flour is essential for the quality of the pastry and cakes I prefer to make.

When used as a thickening agent cornflour gives a 'cloudy' finish to a soup or sauce. Potato flour or arrowroot will give a 'clear' finish.

## PEPPER

I keep three pepper mills on the go: black for a full-flavoured, warm tone; white, as it is gentler and doesn't leave black specks in a pale soup or sauce; and five corn – black, white, brown, pink and red peppercorns bought ready mixed – for a wonderful aromatic blend to mill over smoked salmon, scrambled eggs or salads.

Green and pink peppers (known as Baies Vertes and Baies Roses) are sold in brine; I prefer the latter – even a half-teaspoonful of green peppercorns dominates an entire dish. Whichever you select, use them sparingly.

## VINEGARS

Malt vinegar should be restricted to the fish and chip shop, where it has its rightful place, and ought never to be seen on a self-respecting cook's kitchen shelf. A good brand of red and white wine vinegar, as well as a good cider vinegar, are essential for salads.

Today there are many 'new' vinegars, such as raspberry, strawberry, sherry, and various herbs. I prefer, though, to use fresh herbs, aromatics and fruit juices in combination with red and white wine vinegars.

## COOKING WINE

Use a reasonably good-quality wine when cooking: particularly white. Use Burgundy-type wines for lighter dishes, or for a fruit dish where red wine is called for.

When cooking with red or white wine, I advise you to reduce the wine by one-third by boiling it rapidly in a stainless steel or non-stick pan (red wine can stain white enamel coatings). Cool the wine before use. Do not do this, however, for marinades, as the acid content of the wine is needed to break down tough fibres in meats, poultry and game.

When a sweet wine is needed, quality does count. I suggest a light Sauternes or Coteaux du Layon. I would only use Champagne for a sorbet. German and German-type wines have no real place in the kitchen, if only because they are too costly.

## LIQUEURS AND SPIRITS

Essential though they are to the flavour of many dishes, liqueurs *are* expensive, so I suggest you build up a stock of miniature bottles and, when you travel to the Continent, use your duty-free allowance to bring back a variety of unusual liqueurs and *eaux-de-vie*.

## ESSENCES

The only synthetic essence I find acceptable is vanilla – even so, I keep a vanilla pod or two in my caster sugar jar. Otherwise, I use 'the real thing': peppermint cordial; Bacardi, Jamaica and demerara rums; the zest of fresh fruits (or home-dried peel). I can never understand why some cooks insist on adding almond essence to almond paste!

All this said, there is now available in this country a series of real essences – tarragon, coffee, pistachio, mint – but they are very powerful and should be used cautiously. If you are in Paris then a trip to Fauchon just behind the Madeleine (next door to Michel Guérard's Cuisine Minceur shop) is to be recommended for exotica like these, and an amazing selection of natural edible food dyes.

## SPICES

The most useful spices to have in your kitchen cupboard (away from sunlight) are:

Mace
Nutmeg
Cinnamon
Cracked or ground black pepper

Share the cost of more expensive or less-used spices with a friend.

## AROMATICS

Onions, chives, shallots, leeks and garlic come under this heading and are indispensable in any kitchen.

## CITRUS FRUITS

The *zest* of these fruits – the outer skin only – contains the aromatic oils which give their individual flavours to a dish. The white pith is the bitter (unwanted) part. Use a potato peeler to remove the zest, taking great care not to cut into the pith. When using a grater, use short, sharp movements on the fine teeth only. Some graters are better than others. Select one which clearly has machine-cut teeth, not one where the teeth appear to have been nail-pierced. These are too vicious.

## STOCK

Those who follow my recipes on *Pebble Mill* or in *Homes and Gardens* will have noticed that I frequently give the choice of using a stock cube instead of fresh stock. It seems to me unrealistic to do otherwise, considering the frenetic life most cooks lead in 1985. If you do use a stock cube, make it weaker than the instructions say, or — for gravies particularly — substitute white or red wine, or sherry, for part of the water. On the whole though, I would advise using a good-quality tinned clear soup (consommé), whether chicken, beef or game.

However, we *do* have the best ingredients in the world, make no mistake about that, though I fear our attitude towards their use is still in question, and if we are to lift English cookery into the realms of the sublime, where it can and ought to be, we must give thought to getting the basics right. Without a good stock, how are you to get a good soup, sauce or gravy? Not from the boiled-up, cloudy, bone-based, stock-pot of yesteryear.

Stocks are *not* cheap to make these days, so I recommend that you make yours in large quantities: you can then freeze small ½ pint (275 ml) amounts for use in recipes as you need them. Follow the basic rules I give in the recipes, and you cannot go wrong. The first — and last — investment you have to make is the purchase of a vast pan — up to 20 pints (11.3 litres) in capacity. This will be a purchase you will never regret. My old Le Creuset pan celebrates its thirty-fourth birthday this year, since I brought it back with me across the Channel in the early 1950s: it has doubled up as jam pan, ham-boiler, party spaghetti cooker, punch bowl, planter, wine cooler, bain-marie and — dare I confess it! — sock-soaker! Cheaper, lightweight pans are all right for stock, but you won't get so many other uses out of them.

Having got your pan, all that is required now is patience, for you need to let the stock make itself.

## HERBS

Rosemary Verey is one of England's authorities on gardens and herb gardens. A letter she wrote to me recently contains concise and practical advice for those wanting to grow their own herbs:

'Thank you for a delicious herby lunch,' wrote a friend. Her remark delighted me for herbs, fresh and dried, are essential ingredients in my cooking. For starters we had had the red stems of ruby chard with handfuls of parsley chopped into melted butter, lamb seasoned with rosemary, mint sauce and chervil on the new potatoes.

Our herb bed is immediately outside the kitchen door — in my opinion the best place for it so I can slip out, even in the dark, to collect a handful of flavours. Please do not be deterred by lack of ground, herbs are accommodating — they will grow well in tubs and containers, so the enthusiastic cook with a tiny garden or only a window box can still have her selection.

These are the herbs I find most useful and a little about the way we grow and use them. First there are those which keep their leaves in winter.

Rosemary loves a well-drained place in the sun; the strongly aromatic leaves give a subtle flavour to lamb and to egg dishes. Add a bay leaf to your rice pudding and put one or two inside baked trout. Bay leaves are a traditional ingredient of the bouquet garni, together with thyme and parsley. Sage is strong tasting so use it sparingly, chopped into an omelette or used with cheese. It is a good feature for the centre of your tub on the patio. There are several varieties of thyme and they will look well surrounding your bay and sage.

There are several favourite perennials. They die down in winter so you must pick, dry and store their leaves for winter use. Mint is my first choice. Chop it finely for mint sauce, sprinkle it over potatoes and use it as flavouring in thick soup. The aroma of mint cooking is delicious. In the garden do not let its roots infiltrate into your choice plants. You can dig a few roots in autumn, lay them in a box or pot and put them in the cool house and you will be surprised on a January day to find tender young shoots appearing. Chives are versatile – they are good for soups, omelettes, salads and may be chopped into cream cheese. They are useful in the garden too if you use them as an edging. To bring a clump on in early spring, put a glass jar over a small patch and new growth will quickly start.

Marjoram is a must, and if you use the golden leaf variety it is lovely in the garden too. I use it mostly in meat dishes. Sorrel you need for soup, and lemon balm as a soothing herb tea. Fennel, lovage and angelica make impressive border plants where you need height. Use fennel with fish, a stem of angelica with rhubarb and a leaf of lovage gives soups and sauces a distinct taste of celery. I could do without hyssop in the kitchen, but it has a pretty flower in the autumn. Every good cook loves tarragon, and it must be the French variety. I keep two large flower pots of it and tuck these away for the winter in the cool greenhouse to ensure an early supply. I use it with chicken, tomatoes, baked eggs and runner beans.

Now we get to the annuals and biennials. We sow parsley every spring to keep a supply, you must have enough to cut constantly. Chervil, an annual, is perhaps the Cinderella of herbs and is often neglected. You should use it fresh, for the leaves wilt quickly, but its flavour is rewarding and strong. Dill is an annual which resents being transplanted. The soft feathery leaves are useful for flavouring fish – add it at the last moment. We all know about dill-water given to us in the nursery when we had hiccoughs.

I still have two useful herbs to mention. Coriander is grown for its seed to add to curry and other 'hot' dishes. You can buy the seeds but you must grow basil yourself. I think it is my favourite. Grown each year from seed it will be ready for picking by July just when you are wanting a new and exciting flavour. If you are not sure that all your guests like your choice of herbs on their salad, pick them each a small bunch of mixed herbs and put this in a glass beside their place. Give them some scissors and they can chop their own onto their salad. I could not cook without my herbs!

## *R*OSEMARY VEREY
*Gloucestershire*

### *T*O MAKE A FRESH BOUQUET GARNI

*2 × 4 inch (10 cm) pieces celery*

*2 large sprigs parsley*

*1 small fresh bay leaf*

*1 good sprig thyme*

*1 sprig marjoram*

Place the herbs between the two pieces of celery, and tie with string.

# SOUPS

*In spite of the wide choice of starters available in restaurants, and in the pages of cookery books and magazine food features, soup is still the most popular curtain-raiser to any meal for the great majority of English people.◆For me, the growing popularity and variety of cold, chilled or iced soup (call them by what name you will, as long as they are just that — cold) is the most exciting move since vichyssoise first crossed the Channel.◆Food processors and blenders have taken all the labour out of soup-making: it only remains for me to encourage you to make good stocks and use the freshest of ingredients, to keep the combination of ingredients simple, and the portions moderate!*

# *B*ASIC RICH
## BROWN BEEF STOCK

*3 lb (1.4 kg) mixed marrowbones and others, sawn in manageable pieces*

*3 lb (1.4 kg) shin of beef, trimmed of all fat, cut into 2 inch (5 cm) pieces*

*2 tbsp olive or soy oil*

*8 oz (225 g) carrot, peeled and sliced*

*4 oz (110 g) onion, unskinned, cut in half*

*1 leek, trimmed and roughly chopped*

*4 oz (110 g) 'field' or flat-cap mushrooms*

*2 sticks celery, trimmed and sliced*

*1 pint (570 ml) burgundy-type red wine*

*A fresh bouquet garni or 2 commercial sachets*

*1 lb (450 g) tomatoes, skinned, seeded and chopped*

*1 tsp salt*

*1 tsp black peppercorns, whole*

*5–6 pints (2.8–3.4 litres) cold water*

Preheat the oven to gas mark 9, 475°F (240°C). Place the bones in a roasting tin and brown at this high heat, turning them with tongs to ensure they are well coloured. This can take 45 minutes to an hour.

Remove the bones and place on one side on a tray. Transfer the roasting tin to the top of the stove and brown the shin in the residue fats on all sides, over a fierce heat, working with a manageable batch at a time.

In a soup pan, heat 2 tablespoons of olive oil until smoking. Add the carrots and celery and brown over a high heat, stirring to ensure even colouring and no burning. Lower the heat to almost minimal. Add the bones, meat and all the other ingredients, covering with sufficient cold water. (Discard any fatty residues that are left after browning the bones and meat.)

In order to extract all the goodness from the bones and meat, bring to the boil very slowly. The stock must be actually boiling, not just simmering, but be careful as a rapid boil will cloud things. Add the browned onion pieces (see below).

Cook, uncovered, for 3 hours, skimming off any dirt or scum which rises to the surface during this lengthy process.

Cool. Decant the stock through a lined sieve as for chicken stock (p. 23). Cool completely, then chill overnight.

*To brown the onion*

Slice an onion in two and place, cut-face down, in a dry frying pan on a low heat, or on top of an Aga hotplate. Allow it to brown gently but completely. It should be caramelised but not burnt.

*Note* The shin beef can be used up in a 'cheap and cheerful' chilli or curry.

# *R*ICH
## GAME STOCK

*P*ROCEED exactly as for the beef stock, substituting 3 lb (1.4 kg) bony shoulder of venison for the shin of beef and adding a large sprig of fresh sage, 1 teaspoon of coriander seeds and 1 teaspoon of juniper berries to the pot.

### *T*O MAKE GAME CONSOMMÉ

Use 3 pints (1.75 litres) of game stock with the clarification given for the beef consommé. For a truly gamey consommé, substitute a cheap cut of venison, minced, in place of the minced beef.

Finish the consommé by adding 2 fluid ounces (50 ml) of dry port or Madeira per pint (570 ml) of consommé.

# *C*LEAR SOUP

*C*ONSOMMÉ is now the accepted anglicised term for clear soup, or 'transparent' soup as it was called in England for many centuries. With today's trend for slimmer, healthier eating, it makes a very elegant starter to any meal. But it can be insipid: hence the wealth of interesting ingredients called for not only in the stock recipe just given, but in the clarification method as well. Chicken and fish stocks may be clarified by adding only egg whites, but beef consommé calls for extra minced beef and vegetables to give body, tone, strength of flavour and colour to the soup.

## CLARIFICATION
(for 3 pints (1.75 litres) brown stock)

*1 lb (450 g) minced lean shin of beef*
*1 leek, trimmed and cut into ¼ inch (0.5 cm) dice*
*1 carrot, peeled, and cut into ¼ inch (0.5 cm) dice*
*1 tbsp tomato purée*
*12 white peppercorns*
*1 tsp salt*
*4 fl oz (100 ml) cold water*
*6 egg whites, beaten lightly with a fork to slacken them*

Mix the minced meat, the raw, diced vegetables, tomato purée, pepper-corns, salt and water together. Chill overnight. When ready to make the clear soup, mix the slackened egg whites into the mince mixture. Pour over the chilled beef stock. Transfer the mixture to a soup pan – or do the whole operation in this from the start.

Stand the pan over a *low* heat, and stir until it comes to the boil. Patience here is essential. Rapid boiling will cloud the consommé. As soon as things reach a steady boil stop stirring. Draw the pan to the side of the heat, so that the stock keeps rolling gently. Leave it like this for 45 minutes to 1 hour, when it will be crystal-clear. Turn off the heat and leave the stock – now consommé – to cool completely, before decanting as for chicken stock.

# $B$ASIC CHICKEN STOCK

*1 × 3 lb (1.4 kg) chicken (or boiling fowl)*
*1½–2 lb (700–900 g) knuckle of veal, chopped into manageable pieces*
*4 oz (110 g) carrot, peeled and sliced*
*2 large leeks (white part only), trimmed, washed and finely sliced*
*2 stalks celery, trimmed and sliced*
*4 oz (110 g) white-cap mushrooms, rubbed clean and sliced*
*1 bouquet garni sachet*
*1 tbsp butter or soy oil*
*1 pint (570 ml) dry white wine*
*3 pints (1.75 litres) or more cold water*
*2 tsp salt*
*12 white peppercorns*

Melt the butter without browning it. Add the carrots, leeks and celery, cover with a lid and soften them over a low heat, without browning, for 12–15 minutes.

Add the chicken, knuckle pieces, mushrooms and bouquet garni. Pour the wine and water over to cover. Add the salt and peppercorns. Bring to the boil *slowly*. Adjust the heat so that the liquid is boiling, but only gently so. Rapid boiling creates a cloudy stock.

Boil at this gentle pace for 2 hours, taking the chicken out after 1½ hours and skimming the surface of any dirt which may collect. Cool, then decant the clear stock into a large bowl through a sieve lined with clean muslin or kitchen paper.

Be patient, let the stock trickle through at its own pace: do not be tempted to press it through. Change the paper, or rinse the muslin from time to time to rid it of any sediments.

Chill until ready for use. Under normal good refrigeration, this stock will keep for 7–10 days, or you can freeze it in appropriate quantities.

*Note*   Use up the chicken or boiling fowl in a mayonnaise, or in a chicken and pasta salad. It will curry well, too.

# $R$ICH
## CHICKEN STOCK

*1 × 4 lb (1.8 kg) fresh chicken*

*1 knuckle of veal, washed and cut up*

*4 sticks celery*

*1 medium onion, peeled and quartered*

*1 small head fennel, cleaned and quartered*

*2 medium carrots, peeled and sliced*

*2 cloves garlic, peeled, left whole*

*2 bouquet garni sachets*

*1 pint (570 ml) dry white wine*

*4 pints (2.3 litres) cold water*

*2 tsp whole white peppercorns*

Put the chicken and veal knuckle into a large pan. Pack all the other ingredients round, then cover with the wine and cold water. Bring to the boil slowly as you want to extract all the flavours into the stock. Simmer for

1¼–1½ hours. Remove the chicken. Continue boiling the stock for a further 20 minutes. Strain through a lined sieve. When it is cool skim off all the fats, and refrigerate until ready for use.

In the summer months chicken stock can 'turn' almost whilst you're looking at it. So stand the pan or bowl of strained stock in a sink, with cold water running gently all round it, and stir the stock to ensure even cooling.

Skin and bone the chicken, and cut the meat into bite-size striplets. Refrigerate, covered with plastic film, for use in another dish.

# STRONG FISH STOCK

*The bones from 2 large Dover sole, well washed and cut up (turbot or halibut bones are a suitable alternative)*

*1 large leek, washed and sliced*

*1 carrot, peeled and sliced*

*1 large sprig parsley (a small handful)*

*3 pints (1.75 litres) cold water*

*1 bottle dry white wine*

*1 bouquet garni sachet*

*2 tsp fennel seeds*

*2 dozen white (or black) peppercorns*

*No salt at this stage*

Put all the ingredients into a pan, cover with the water and wine. Bring to the boil slowly, reduce the heat to a minimum and simmer for 1 hour, skimming carefully throughout the cooking time. Leave to cool completely before decanting through a fine sieve lined with either kitchen paper or a clean napkin. Chill well.

## *T*O MAKE CLEAR FISH BROTH
### *or*
### FISH CONSOMMÉ

Allow 2 small egg whites per measured pint (570 ml) of chilled fish stock. Beat these up with a fork without creating too much froth: they should just be well slackened.

Whisk into the chilled stock and bring to the boil very slowly, stirring regularly with a balloon whisk. As soon as boiling point is reached, draw the pan to one side and lower the heat to a minimum: just enough to keep the stock rolling very gently.

Leave to simmer like this *without stirring again* until the stock is quite clear, about 30–35 minutes, and a thick solid scum has formed. Turn off the heat and leave the now clear soup to cool.

Decant through a paper-lined sieve into a clean receptacle: reserve until ready for use.

# *T*OMATO AND PLUM SOUP

*Serves 5–6*

*T*HIS soup is bright red and tastes very fresh. Serve hot or chilled.

*2 oz (50 g) onion, skinned, chopped*

*1 fl oz (25 ml) olive oil*

*1 lb (450 g) red plums, stoned*

*1 lb (450 g) tomatoes, deseeded*

*½ pint (275 ml) fresh tomato juice*

*1 pint (570 ml) chicken stock*

*1 sprig fresh thyme*

*1 tsp caster sugar*

*Salt and milled pepper*

## *T*O GARNISH

*2 plums, stoned and diced*

*1 level tbsp finely chopped parsley*

*1 level tbsp finely snipped chives*

Soften the onion in the oil without colouring it. Add all the remaining ingredients. Bring to the boil and simmer until the fruit is soft (about 12–15 minutes). Cool a little, then blend and rub through a fine sieve.

Reheat or chill. Serve with a spoonful of the mixed garnish.

# CLEAR MUSHROOM BROTH

*Serves 4*

MUSHROOM essences and mushroom katsup (or ketchup) have been a part of the English culinary scene for centuries, although they have fallen into disuse since the turn of this one with the advent of Oxo, and more recently the stock cube.

This exquisite new broth is a timely reminder of how excellent and fitting mushrooms are to the English palate. Serve in smallish cups with perhaps a cheese straw or a couple of lightly buttered fingers of brown toast as an accompaniment.

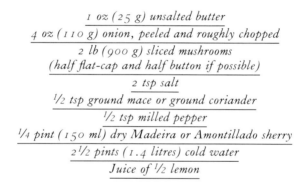

*1 oz (25 g) unsalted butter*

*4 oz (110 g) onion, peeled and roughly chopped*

*2 lb (900 g) sliced mushrooms
(half flat-cap and half button if possible)*

*2 tsp salt*

*½ tsp ground mace or ground coriander*

*½ tsp milled pepper*

*¼ pint (150 ml) dry Madeira or Amontillado sherry*

*2½ pints (1.4 litres) cold water*

*Juice of ½ lemon*

## TO GARNISH

*1 oz (25 g) white button mushrooms, finely sliced and quickly browned in
¼ oz (5 g) sizzling butter*

*2 or 3 coriander leaves if you can lay your hands on some*

or

*1 oz (25 g) wild or brown rice, boiled and rinsed as per instructions on the packet*

Melt the butter in a large pan until foaming. Add the onion, stirring in well, lower the heat and cook, covered, until soft. Add the mushrooms and all the remaining ingredients. Cover with the water, bring to the boil slowly and cook at a good simmer for 1½ hours. Cool. Strain through a heavy felt jellybag for a clear broth. (A couple of clean white felt squares lining a sieve will do quite well if you don't have a jellybag. These should be washed afterwards in biological powder, rinsed, soaked in cold water overnight, rinsed again and dried.) Discard the mushroom pulp which will have had all the goodness cooked out of it.

To serve, reheat the broth to boiling point. Warm soup cups or tea cups and rinse them with a teaspoon of sherry or Madeira. Add 2 or 3 slivers of mushroom or 1 teaspoonful of cooked rice to each cup.

# CREAMY WHITE TURNIP SOUP

*Serves 4*

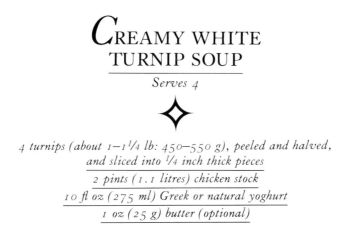

4 *turnips (about 1–1¼ lb: 450–550 g), peeled and halved, and sliced into ¼ inch thick pieces*

2 *pints (1.1 litres) chicken stock*

10 *fl oz (275 ml) Greek or natural yoghurt*

1 *oz (25 g) butter (optional)*

Cook the turnips in the chicken stock until quite soft. Drain, retaining the liquor. Pass the turnips through a food processor or blender (for once there's no necessity to rub the purée through a fine sieve!).

Mix the yoghurt well in, add the knob of butter if used, and reheat, adding enough of the cooking liquor from the turnips to give a texture like single cream. And that's it!

The soup is delicious served chilled, in which case do not add too much of the liquor, but add a good pouring of double cream to enrich the soup even further.

# CHILLED BEETROOT SOUP

*Serves 6*

*T*HE deep, sweet fruity flavour of the beetroot is wonderfully offset by the sharpness of buttermilk, unhampered by any strong spices. If you find it difficult to obtain buttermilk – and do try health-food shops – use natural yoghurt. A mixture of half natural yoghurt and half single cream will give a richer version for you to try for a summer lunch party.

*1½ lb (700 g) beetroot, weighed after boiling and skinning*
*1¼ pints (700 ml) chicken stock*
*1 tsp salt*
*2 tbsp lemon juice (1 small lemon)*
*10 fl oz (275 ml) buttermilk, or a mixture of natural yoghurt and single cream*
*1 heaped tbsp finely snipped chives*

Cut the beetroot into small pieces and purée in a food processor or blender, using the stock as liquid. Press through a fine-meshed sieve. Season with the salt and lemon juice, whisk in the buttermilk or yoghurt and cream. Chill well.

Serve with plenty of snipped chives to each serving.

# CLEAR FISH BROTH
# WITH SEAFOOD AND FENNEL

*Serves 4*

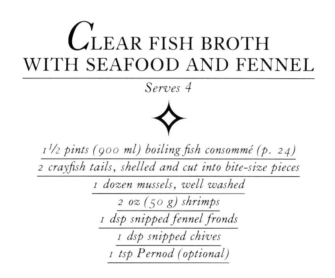

*1½ pints (900 ml) boiling fish consommé (p. 24)*
*2 crayfish tails, shelled and cut into bite-size pieces*
*1 dozen mussels, well washed*
*2 oz (50 g) shrimps*
*1 dsp snipped fennel fronds*
*1 dsp snipped chives*
*1 tsp Pernod (optional)*

Place the mussels in a steamer and steam until opened (about 7–8 minutes). Take out of their shells.

Distribute between four hot soup cups or plates, together with the other ingredients, including the Pernod, if used.

Ladle over the boiling consommé, which will suffice to heat the crayfish without toughening it.

*Note* If Pernod is used, then you need only use fish *stock* as this liqueur makes all liquids go milky, making a crystal-clear soup superfluous.

# CHILLED SMOKED SALMON SOUP WITH SMOKED TROUT

*Serves 4*

*A* LUXURY soup, very rich, and to be served in chilled soup cups, using a small dessertspoon to eat it with, in place of the larger soup spoon. This may seem a fine point, but it's one well worth bearing in mind.

*10 oz (275 g) Scottish smoked salmon*
*³/4 pint (400 ml) cold fish stock (p. 24)*
*³/4 pint (400 ml) single cream*
*Juice of ¹/2 small lemon*
*Milled white pepper*

### TO GARNISH

*1 smoked trout, skinned, boned, and carefully flaked into its natural flakes*
*1 tbsp very finely snipped chives or spring onion*

Make a fine purée of the smoked salmon and the fish stock. Rub through a fine sieve. Stir in the cream (adjust the consistency if necessary with strained fish stock — the thickness of cream varies throughout the country). Add the lemon juice and pepper, and chill well.

Divide the garnish equally between the soup cups. Sprinkle with snipped chives or spring onions.

# POTATO CREAM SOUP

*Serves 4*

*A* TRUE potato flavour comes through in this soup, reminiscent of a robust soup of yesteryear, and yet possessing an elegance of its own.

I don't consider a garnish necessary, other than meticulously cut mini balls of potato. These are made using a 'Solferino' scoop obtainable from any good cookshop.

*1 oz (25 g) butter*
*3 medium leeks, white part only, sliced*
*1 clove garlic, crushed*
*1 lb (450 g) potatoes, peeled, and cut into ½ inch (1 cm) dice*
*1 pint (570 ml) chicken stock (p. 22)*
*½ pint (275 ml) double cream*
*Salt only (black pepper mars the delicate colour of the soup)*
*1 large potato for garnish (see method)*

Melt the butter without browning it. Over a low heat soften the leeks in it with the garlic in a lidded pan. Add the potatoes and stock. Simmer until quite soft.

Blend or liquidise the vegetables, and then rub the soup through a fine-meshed sieve. Cool, then chill.

For a cold soup, chill the cups first, and stir in chilled cream just before serving. To serve hot, bring to the boil slowly in a non-stick pan, adding the cream as you go along. The soup should be of the consistency of good pouring cream.

Make the potato ball garnish by scooping out mini balls of potato, or cut into ¼ inch (0.5 cm) dice, and rinse in a bowl of cold water. Cook for 2–3 minutes in a pan of boiling lightly salted water. Alternatively, to add a bit of colour, sprinkle finely snipped chives or fresh parsley over the surface of each serving.

# CHILLED HERB GARDEN SOUP

*Serves 4–6*

A VARIATION of the previous recipe, this is a summer soup for when your herb plot (or window boxes) are at their most prolific.

Proceed as for Potato Cream Soup above, chilling the soup well overnight. On the day of serving, add the following freshly picked herbs which should be very finely chopped.

*1 level tbsp of each:*
*Flat-leafed or curly parsley*
*Applemint*
*Borage*
*Fennel fronds or tarragon (not both)*
*Chives*
*Garlic*

I have suggested a fine balance of herbs and aromatics: allowing the flavour of each room to expand, so to speak, so that no two clash with each other.

# $R$ICH CREAM OF VEGETABLE SOUP

*Serves 4–6*

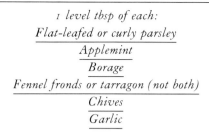

$T$HIS soup has a light thickening of egg yolks and cream, instead of a heavier flour and butter thickening so often used in the past.

*1 1/2 pints (900 ml) rich chicken stock (p. 23)*
*A little lemon juice*
*1 courgette*
*1 carrot, peeled*
*1/2 cucumber, deseeded*
*2 oz (50 g) frozen baby peas (defrosted)*
*1/4 cauliflower, cut into minuscule florets*
*1 small turnip, peeled*
*1/2 pint (275 ml) single cream*
*4 egg yolks*

Clean and cut the vegetables into shapes or balls, using cutting spoons, or cut into 1/4 inch (0.5 cm) dice.

Bring the stock to the boil. Adjust the seasoning, adding 2 teaspoons or so of lemon juice. Toss in the vegetables and cook for 2–3 minutes, so that they are still crisp. Strain, and put the vegetables into a tureen to keep warm.

Mix the egg yolks with the cream, stir into the hot soup over a minimal heat until the soup thickens *slightly*. Pour over the vegetables, serve with fingers of choux pastry (see p. 217) filled with cottage cheese.

# CREAM OF MUSSEL SOUP WITH SAFFRON

*Serves 4*

2 pints (1.1 litres) fresh mussels, well washed
½ pint (275 ml) strong fish stock (p. 24)
½ pint (275 ml) double cream
2 sachets 'Zaffy' saffron powder
1 tbsp dry sherry
1 tsp white peppercorns
3 egg yolks
A little lemon juice

In a large pan bring the stock to a rolling boil. Tip in the cleaned mussels, cover, then shake and toss them over a high heat until the shells have opened (about 5 minutes). Discard *any* unopened ones. Drain, retaining the liquid. Strain this through a muslin-lined sieve to rid it of bits of stray shell.

Shell the mussels, de-beard them, and set aside, covered with a wetted cloth, whilst you finish the soup. Return the liquids to a pan, add the sherry, and the saffron and cream mixed together, reserving a little to mix with the egg yolks. Simmer for 5 minutes, adjust the seasoning with salt, milled pepper and a squeeze of lemon juice. Divide the mussels between warmed soup cups. Remove the boiling soup from the heat, whisk in the egg yolks and cream mixture. Ladle over the mussels and serve immediately.

# CREAM OF CARROT SOUP

*Serves 4–6*

RESIST the temptation to add any extra ingredient to this elegant soup, such as orange, ginger, parsley or bouquet garni. Let the refined carrot flavour speak for itself. Serve chilled or hot, in smallish quantities.

*Page 33 Clear Mushroom Broth    Page 34 Rich Cream of Vegetable Soup*

*1 lb (450 g) carrots, weighed after peeling*
*8 oz (225 g) white part of leek, shredded*
*½ pint (275 ml) chicken stock (see p. 22)*
*½ pint (275 ml) single cream*

## MACE BUTTER

*2 oz (50 g) butter, softened*
*Juice of ½ lemon*
*Salt and milled pepper*
*1 level tsp ground mace*

Cut the carrots into discs, put into a pan with the leeks, cover with the stock and simmer until completely tender.

Cool, purée in a food processor, then rub completely through a fine-meshed sieve. Stir in the cream. Chill well.

If served hot, reheat and hand round a savoury mace butter separately for each guest to stir in at will: beat or blend all the ingredients for the butter to a soft paste. Using a teaspoon dipped into hot water, scoop small knobs onto a piece of greaseproof paper. Put to set in the freezer until ready to serve. Alternatively, press the butter into a small pot and serve lightly chilled but still spoonable.

# CHILLED SPINACH AND WATERCRESS SOUP

*Serves 5–6*

*I*T is essential that this soup is a vivid green.

*12 oz (350 g) fresh spinach, to yield 8 oz (225 g) cooked, drained and puréed*
*3 bundles watercress, picked of main stalks and fibres, and washed*
*½ pint (275 ml) rich chicken stock (or tinned chicken consommé)*
*½ pint (275 ml) single cream*
*1 tbsp finely snipped chives or the middle part of young spring onions*
*1 tbsp finely chopped parsley*

Mix the spinach and watercress together. In a large lidded pan, bring to the boil 2 inches (5 cm) of lightly salted water. Put in the spinach and watercress, cover and boil rapidly for 2 minutes, when the spinach will be wilted. Drain, and rinse under running water until cold. Drain again, and make a fine purée in a blender or food processor. Stir in half the chicken stock and all the cream, adding more stock to reach a consistency of pouring cream. Stir in the chives and parsley, and chill well.

If you want to make a hot soup, and retain the all-essential bright green colour, then proceed as follows: in a large pan, bring to the boil slowly ⅔ of the chicken stock and the cream. Then – and only then – stir in the spinach and watercress purée, a little at a time. Adjust the consistency, add the chives and parsley, and serve straightaway. If the soup is allowed to stand for any length of time, it will lose its colour and go beige.

# 'LONDON PARTICULAR'
## (Rich Pea Soup)

*Serves 4*

*A* SOUP which took its name from the famous fogs which once blanketed our capital city: or perhaps it was the other way around. Whichever it was, I have redesigned this pea-souper to slot into any of your party menus at any time – noon or night, winter or summer, chilly and cool or sultry and hot.

*1 oz (25 g) butter or oil*

*1 bunch spring onions, trimmed and shredded*

*1 clove garlic, crushed*

*10 oz (275 g) frozen baby peas (defrosted)*

*1 pint (570 ml) chicken stock (see p. 22)*

*1 'flat' lettuce, washed, trimmed and roughly cut up*

*1 tsp caster sugar*

*Salt and milled pepper to taste*

## OPTIONAL GARNISHES

*2 tbsp freshly chopped mint, stirred in when the soup is cold*

*1 heaped tsp minced lean smoked ham per serving*

Melt the butter, add the onions and garlic. Cover, and soften over a low heat without colouring (about 3–4 minutes). Add the peas and cold stock. Add the sugar and season well. Bring to the boil, simmer for 5 minutes. Add the lettuce after 3 minutes. Cool a little, then pass through a blender or food processor. For a very elegant soup, rub through a fine-meshed sieve as well. The consistency should be that of rich pouring cream.

To retain a good colour, stand the soup in a sink of iced water to cool completely. Pea soup discolours very quickly. (If this happens, *one* drop of edible food colouring is permitted as a cosmetic aid.) Chill. Garnish to taste before serving. If served hot, reheat quickly, stirring all the time, and serve immediately.

# *M*USHROOM, TOMATO, ORANGE AND WALNUT SOUP

*Serves 4–6*

*D*ARK-toned and tweedy in texture, this is an ideal main-course soup.

*12 oz (350 g) flat black-cap mushrooms*

*1 clove garlic, crushed*

*1 oz (25 g) butter or oil*

*Up to 1 pint (570 ml) rich beef stock (p. 20), or chicken stock (p. 22)*

*2 fl oz (50 ml) Amontillado sherry*

*½ pint (275 ml) tomato pulp made from 1 lb tomatoes, skinned, seeded and roughly chopped*

*¼ pint (150 ml) fresh orange juice*

*¼ tsp finely grated orange rind*

*Salt and milled white pepper to taste*

## GARNISH

*1 orange, segmented with a knife*

*1 tomato, skinned, seeded, cut into petals*

*2 oz (50 g) walnuts, toasted, lightly salted and roughly crushed*

*(These can all be made a day in advance.)*

Trim the stalk ends and peel the mushrooms. Chop roughly.

Melt the butter or oil in a heavy-bottomed pan until foaming and almondy. Add the mushrooms and garlic, toss well and stir over a brisk heat until the juices begin to draw. Add all the remaining ingredients, lower the heat, and simmer for 15–20 minutes.

Allow to cool before blending – but do not over-blend: a somewhat tweedy texture is preferable. Reheat and serve with a little of each garnish stirred into each cup.

# $O$XTAIL SOUP
# WITH CHESTNUTS

*Serves 4–6*

*1 oxtail, 2–2½ lb (900 g–1.1 kg) in weight*

*1 tbsp white flour*

*2 tbsp soy oil*

*1 lamb's tongue*

*1 leek, trimmed and sliced*

*1 onion, chopped*

*1 carrot, peeled and diced*

*2 sticks celery, diced*

*1 lb (450 g) tomatoes, skinned, seeded and chopped*

*2 pints (1.1 litres) beef stock (or tinned consommé)*

*¼ pint (150 ml) dry sherry, Amontillado type*

*6–8 sage leaves*

*1 sprig thyme*

*1 clove garlic, crushed*

*½ tsp ground mace*

*1 tbsp redcurrant jelly*

*1 tsp ground ginger*

*1 level tbsp dark muscovado sugar*

*Salt and pepper*

## $C$HESTNUT GARNISH

*2 chestnuts in brine, drained, per serving*

*½ fl oz (10 ml) olive oil*

*1 tsp caster sugar*

Toss the pieces of oxtail in flour in a plastic bag. Preheat the oven to gas mark 9, 475°F (240°C). In a roasting tin heat the oil until smoking. Add the oxtail and roast this until well browned, moving and turning the pieces every 5 minutes or so.

Remove the pieces, then brown the leek, onion, carrot and celery well in the remaining oil, adding an extra tablespoonful if necessary. Transfer the oxtail and vegetables together to a large pan. Add all the remaining ingredients, including the lamb's tongue, discarding any excess oils.

Bring to the boil slowly, lower the heat and simmer for 2–2½ hours, or until the oxtail meat leaves the bones readily. Cool, then strain through a sieve. Skim off any oils which rise to the surface using a small ladle or table-spoon. Strip the meat from the oxtail and dice it. Adjust the seasoning of the soup. Prepare the chestnuts for the garnish: heat the oil until smoking. Add the sugar and allow to caramelise. Toss the chestnuts in the caramel to coat them, and heat them through. Reheat the soup, then add the diced meat. Garnish with the chestnuts. This soup should have a very light texture.

# MULLIGATAWNY

*Serves 4*

*1 raw chicken breast, skinned*

*½ oz (10 g) butter*

*2 pints (1.1 litres) rich chicken stock (p. 23)*

*2 oz (50 g) pudding rice, washed*

*½ tsp Madras curry paste (or to taste)*

*1 oz (25 g) sultanas plumped in 1 tbsp light rum*

*2 dsp desiccated coconut*

*1 tbsp coriander leaves, roughly chopped (or flat-leafed parsley)*

Cut the chicken breast into the thinnest striplets you can. Melt the butter in a large pan, and fry the chicken for 1 minute. Stir in the small amount of curry paste and the rice.

Cover with the stock and simmer for 20 minutes, when the rice will be tender. Add the remaining ingredients, reheat and serve.

# CHRISTMAS (OR POMPION) SOUP

## Serves 4

*P*OMPION was the eighteenth-century word for a pumpkin. This is a rich warm-toned soup which combines all the autumn flavours, and may be served hot or chilled.

*4 oz (110 g) onion, skinned and chopped*

*1 oz (25 g) butter or olive oil*

*1 small clove garlic, crushed*

*12 oz (350 g) cubed pumpkin (or melon), weighed after peeling and deseeding*

*6 oz (175 g) freshly boiled and skinned chestnuts, or chestnuts in brine, strained*

*1 stock cube, crumbled*

*2 × 2 inch (5 cm) slivers orange rind*

*1 tsp ground ginger*

*1 tsp mild sweet paprika*

*1 level tsp milled white or black pepper*

*1 tsp salt (or to taste)*

*1 'envelope' saffron powder (optional)*

*1 pint (570 ml) fresh or carton of orange juice*

*½ pint (275 ml) single cream (optional for dieters)*

### OPTIONAL GARNISHES

*½ a cooked chestnut per helping*

*1 or 2 orange segments per helping*

Melt the butter and fry the onion over a low heat till transparent. Add the garlic and pumpkin or melon. Stir round, cooking gently until the juices 'draw'. Now add all the remaining ingredients and simmer, covered, until the pumpkin is tender. Pass through a mouli or blender, and then rub through a fine sieve. Cool, chill. Just before serving, mix in the chilled cream and garnish to taste. To serve hot, bring the soup to boiling point, stir in the cream, then bring back to just under boiling point. If the cream is omitted, thin the soup down to a light consistency by adding chicken stock, chilled or hot as the case may be.

# COCK-A-LEEKIE

*Serves 4*

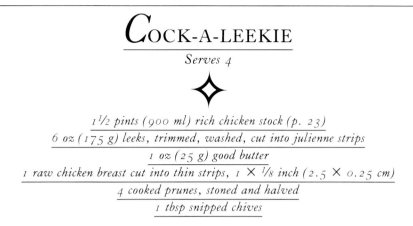

*1½ pints (900 ml) rich chicken stock (p. 23)*

*6 oz (175 g) leeks, trimmed, washed, cut into julienne strips*

*1 oz (25 g) good butter*

*1 raw chicken breast cut into thin strips, 1 × ⅛ inch (2.5 × 0.25 cm)*

*4 cooked prunes, stoned and halved*

*1 tbsp snipped chives*

Melt the butter in a pan without browning it. Cook the chicken strips in this for 5 minutes. Remove with a slotted spoon to a plate, until ready for use.

Put the leeks into the residual juices, cover with a lid and sweat for a minute, shaking the pan occasionally. They should still be quite crisp.

Pour the stock over, reheat, and serve sprinkled with the chives and with a prune in each bowl.

# *CHILLED APPLE, GINGER AND MUSTARD SOUP*

*Serves 8*

*2 tbsp soy or olive oil*

*4 oz (110 g) onion, chopped*

*1 clove garlic, crushed*

*1 lb (450 g) Bramleys, cored but not peeled*

*2 heaped tsp dry mustard*

*2 tsp powdered ginger*

*1 bouquet garni*

*2 tsp sugar*

*Juice of 1 lemon*

*1 tsp salt*

*1½ pints (900 ml) chicken stock (or tinned chicken consommé)*

## *TO* GARNISH

*¹/4 pint ( 1 50 ml) single cream*
*1 good piece of stem ginger, finely diced*
*1 Cox's apple, peeled, cut in ¹/8 inch ( 0 . 2 5 cm) dice ( or shredded),*
*tossed in lemon juice*

Heat the oil, then reduce heat and soften the onion in it without letting it take on any colour. Add the garlic, stirring in well, and fry for a second or two. Stir in the mustard and ginger and continue to fry for a few seconds longer.

Add the apples, sugar, salt, lemon juice and stock. Add the bouquet garni, and simmer, covered, until the apples have fallen (about 10 minutes). Cool, then pass through a food processor before rubbing through a fine-meshed sieve. Chill.

Just before serving in chilled soup cups, stir in the chilled cream and sprinkle the garnish over the top of each serving.

# STARTERS

✦

*The key to good entertaining is the element of surprise — you might call it the 'gosh factor'. It can, of course, come later on in the menu, if you are skilful with your main courses; or you can save it for the finale when you bring on an irresistible pudding with a flourish.* ✦ *But I prefer to begin with an indication of what guests might well expect to follow. A simple starter ought to spell out that bigger and greater things are on the way: an elaborate first course should give a hint that the rest of the dishes will, or ought to be, less rich.* ✦ *If you choose to serve an exotic first course, you should plan to round off the meal with something simple like liqueur-soaked berries or pieces of iced fruit.*

# *P*OTTED CRAB
# WITH ORANGES

*Serves 4*

*I* DOUBT that any potted food can be made richer or finer than this without losing the spirit of the name! Orange and crab make a perfect union.

*8 oz (225 g) dressed crab (light and dark meat)*

*5 oz (150 g) unsalted butter*

*2 tbsp Amontillado sherry*

*Juice and rind of 1 small orange*

*¹/₄ tsp salt*

*¹/₈ tsp milled pepper*

## *C*LARIFIED ORANGE BUTTER

*1 tsp grated zest only of 1 orange*

*1¹/₂ oz (40 g) unsalted butter*

## *T*O GARNISH

*2 Jaffa or navel oranges, knife-segmented*

Cut the butter into ½ inch (1 cm) cubes and leave at room temperature. Bring the sherry and orange juice to the boil in a small pan. Boil rapidly until reduced to 1 tablespoonful.

Remove the pan from the heat and, using a small balloon whisk, vigorously beat in the softened butter until it is creamy. Incorporate and beat in the two crab meats. Season well. Press and rub through a fine-meshed metal sieve.

Spoon into 4 individual ramekins. Rap each of them sharply on the table-top to level off (the mixture is soft). Put to set in the refrigerator for 30 minutes, then spoon over a little clarified orange butter to seal the tops. To make this, put the butter with the orange zest and 2 tablespoons of water into a small pan. Bring slowly to the boil, then turn off the heat, and pour and rub the melted butter through a small sieve into a teacup. Put to set in the refrigerator. Remove the circle of 'set' butter, pat and wipe clean on the underside with kitchen paper, then in a clean teacup standing in a basin of hot water melt the butter to a 'cool' melt before spooning over the crab in the ramekins.

This dish can be made one or two days in advance, but should be taken from the refrigerator an hour before serving. Serve with dry brown toast or biscuits, and with 2 or 3 orange segments as an accompaniment.

# SMOKED SALMON 'SCONES'

*Serves 8*

I T is well worth going through the different processes to achieve this 'tribute to the Scots': the result is unusual, and the idea can be extended to other ingredients to fit your imagination.

*12 oz (350 g) choux pastry (p. 217)*
*12 oz (350 g) creamy mashed potato (p. 91)*

## SMOKED SALMON PURÉE

*8 oz (225 g) good smoked salmon*
*4 oz (110 g) butter, softened*
*2 tsp lemon juice*
*Milled white pepper (probably no salt as the salmon will be salty enough)*
*3 fl oz (75 ml) half-whipped cream*
*2 oz (50 g) red salmon roe (optional luxury)*

## GARNISH

*8 × 1 oz (25 g) slices smoked salmon*
*8 curly crisp lettuce leaves*
*1 lemon, cut into 8 wedges*
*8 sprigs watercress*

Mix the pastry and mashed potato together well. Put heaped teaspoons on to a lightly buttered baking sheet. Using the back of another teaspoon dipped into milk, press each into a circle 2 inches (5 cm) in diameter. This quantity should make about 2 dozen scones: allow a good inch (2.5 cm) gap between them. Bake at gas mark 6, 400°F (200°C) for 10–15 minutes. Remove to a cooling tray.

Make the filling by blending the salmon, adding the butter bit by bit, and the lemon juice, to make a fine purée. Season whilst blending. Scrape the purée into a bowl. Stir in the cream, changing to a beating motion if the mixture appears too soft. It should be spreadable like a sweet buttercream. Carefully fold in the salmon roe.

Use a sharp knife to split the scones in two, and fill each with a good spoonful (1 oz: 25 g) of the salmon mixture, spooning it onto the base. Sit the top on at a slight angle. Stand the scones on the edge of the lettuce leaves. Tuck a sprig of watercress under the lid and serve each with a thin lemon wedge. Place the slice of smoked salmon attractively alongside, or serve with horseradish cream. Any surplus scones can be stored in an airtight tin and eaten, warmed up, for breakfast.

# SPICED CRAB-STUFFED EGGS

*Serves 6*

*12 eggs, hard-boiled*

*Wholewheat bread or toast*

*6 oz (175 g) butter, softened*

*1 small freshly dressed crab (about 8–10 oz: 225–275 g) weighed after dressing*

*2 oz (50 g) freshly grated Parmesan cheese*

*1 heaped tsp Colman's tarragon mustard*

*2 heaped tsp Baies Roses (pink peppercorns in brine)*

*1 clove garlic, crushed*

*2 good dashes tabasco*

*1 level tsp salt*

*Good squeeze of lemon juice*

*2 heaped tsp tomato purée*

*1 tbsp freshly chopped tarragon (or parsley)*

*1 level tsp milled black pepper*

Cut a small piece off the top and bottom of each egg. Keep the tops. Empty the eggs with an apple corer by gently plunging it down the centre from top to bottom. Put all the filling ingredients plus the hard-boiled egg yolks into a blender or food processor. Mix until smooth. Press through a fine sieve.

Using a large rose tube fitted into a piping bag, pipe the mixture into the eggs. Fit the 'cap' of egg white on top. Spread any remaining mixture on to circles of wholewheat bread or toast. Stand an egg on top of each circle. Serve at room temperature.

# TARTLET OF QUAILS' EGGS WITH COTTAGE CHEESE AND SMOKED SALMON

*Serves 4*

## PASTRY

*6 oz (175 g) plain white flour*

*4 oz (110 g) butter and lard mixed*

*2 oz (50 g) freshly grated Parmesan cheese*

*½ tsp salt and a pinch of cayenne pepper*

*1 egg yolk mixed with 2 tbsp cold water*

## FOR THE FILLING

*Allow per serving:*

*1 oz (25 g) cottage cheese*

*1 oz (25 g) smoked salmon, cut into small dice*

*Salt and milled pepper*

*Squeeze of lemon juice*

## TO GARNISH

*2 quails' eggs, boiled, shelled and cut in half*

*A few juicy capers*

*Snipped chives*

*Paprika*

Prepare the pastry. Rub the fats into the flour. Toss in the cheese, season and mix to a dough with the egg and water. Leave to rest for 30 minutes.

Roll out and cut to fit the buttered *outsides* of tartlet tins placed upside down on a baking tray. Bake at gas mark 5, 375°F (190°C) for 20–25 minutes until the pastry is crisp and a nice pale brown colour. Cool a little. Remove the tins carefully and place the tartlets right side up on a cooling tray. These quantities should yield 10–12 tartlets depending on the size of your particular tins. Freeze or store any you don't use, or freeze the balance of the raw pastry.

Mix the cottage cheese with the lemon juice, salt and pepper for the filling. Mix in the smoked salmon. Chill well.

Fill the baked pastry shells just before serving so that the pastry stays crisp. Sit 4 quails' egg halves on top of each one. Garnish with capers or a sprinkling of snipped chives or paprika.

# $P$OTTED SMOKED TROUT WITH HORSERADISH

*Serves 6*

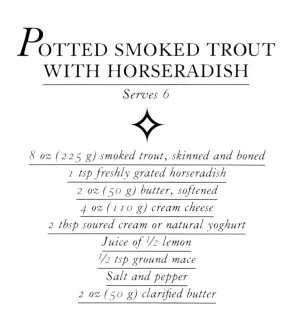

8 oz (225 g) smoked trout, skinned and boned

1 tsp freshly grated horseradish

2 oz (50 g) butter, softened

4 oz (110 g) cream cheese

2 tbsp soured cream or natural yoghurt

Juice of 1/2 lemon

1/2 tsp ground mace

Salt and pepper

2 oz (50 g) clarified butter

Make a fine purée of the smoked trout and horseradish in a blender or food processor. Mix in the remaining ingredients, except the clarified butter, in short, sharp bursts. Rub through a fine-meshed sieve for extra refinement.

Spoon into pretty pots, pour over a film of clarified butter and leave to set. Take out of the refrigerator at least 1 hour before serving. Serve with hot, dry brown toast.

# SCRAMBLED EGGS WITH ROSEMARY

*Serves 1*

*1 oz (25 g) butter*
*2 eggs, lightly beaten and mixed with 1 tbsp cream*
*Salt and milled white pepper*
*1 sprig fresh rosemary, oregano or marjoram*

Melt the butter with the sprig of herb, and leave to infuse in a warm place for 15–20 minutes. Strain into a clean non-stick pan. Over a medium heat and with the butter hot, but not frying hot, pour in the slightly seasoned egg mixture. Each time it sets on the bottom of the pan, use a straight-edged wooden spatula to draw the set egg across, until you have a light creamy mixture, only just set. Excessive heat creates a hard set. Serve in a ramekin with dry toast or crackers.

# TRIPLE PEPPER MOUSSE

*Serves 20*

*T*HIS unusual starter involves a good deal of patience, rather than skill, so you will probably only want to attempt it when entertaining. Obviously the quantities can be halved or divided by three if you wish, or you can make a single pepper mousse only. Try the red one.

There are different ways of skinning peppers: some people plunge them into searing hot deep fat (but if the oil or fat is not clean an unwanted flavour may creep in). Others roast them in a preheated oven – gas mark 9, 475°F (240°C) – to blister them. I choose the somewhat laborious and tedious, but totally controllable, way of doing this job. I spear each one on a cook's fork and blister and char it over a high, naked flame. It can take 6–7 minutes per pepper, so you'll see what I mean by patience. I then wash and peel them under cold running water before halving to remove all seeds and cut away all the pith.

## GREEN PEPPER MOUSSE

*3 green peppers, skinned, deseeded, and with the pith cut away, to yield approx.*
*1/2 pint (275 ml) purée (see method)*

*1 tsp salt*

*1 tbsp snipped chives*

*2 tsp lemon juice*

*6–8 twists of milled white pepper*

*1/3 pint (190 ml) chicken aspic (see method)*

*1/2 pint (275 ml) double cream, whipped to soft peak*

## YELLOW PEPPER MOUSSE

*3 yellow peppers treated as above*

*3 oz (75 g) mango flesh (from 1 medium-sized ripe mango)*

*1/4 tsp ground mace*

*2 tsp lemon juice*

*No salt in this one*

*Grated rind of 1 small orange*

*1/3 pint (190 ml) chicken aspic*

*1/2 pint (275 ml) double cream, whipped to soft peak*

## RED PEPPER MOUSSE

*3 red peppers treated as above*

*1 tsp salt*

*1 tsp sweet paprika*

*2 tsp tomato purée*

*2 dashes tabasco*

*1/3 pint (190 ml) chicken aspic*

*1/2 pint (275 ml) double cream, whipped to soft peak*

## CHICKEN ASPIC

*1 pint (570 ml) strong (double-strength) fresh chicken stock or use 1 1/2 stock cubes to*
*1 pint (570 ml) water*

*3 sachets gelatine crystals*

Bring the stock to the boil. Sprinkle over the gelatine. Remove from heat and stir until fully dissolved. Cool, but do not allow to set.

Make the mousses, using ⅓ pint (190 ml) of the prepared chicken stock as liquid for each one. Make a fine purée of each of the peppers in turn, in a food processor or blender. For a very fine mousse, press the purée through a fine-meshed sieve. Add all the seasonings as you blend.

Scrape the purée into a bowl, whisk and fold in the half-whipped cream, just as the purée is beginning to gel. Pour into individual moulds or proceed as follows if you are going to assemble the party mousse – you will need 2 extra skinned and deseeded red peppers, and a little extra chicken aspic.

Line a 4–5 pint (2.3–2.8 litre) mould, or 2 smaller ones, with a piece of well-oiled greaseproof paper. Float a thin layer of aspic (about 1⁄16 inch: 0.1 cm) in the bottom. Put to set in the refrigerator. Cut the extra red peppers into pieces to fit the base of the mould: float over a further thin layer of aspic and put to set again.

Ladle or pour in the first mousse. Give the mould a sharp bang on the table if it is beginning to gel, in order to level things. Put to set. Ladle over the second mousse, set again: finally ladle over the last mousse and cover with plastic film and leave to set completely, ideally overnight. Use your artistic judgement to decide the order of the stripes of colour.

Unmould by running a hot palette knife round the sides of the mould. Invert onto a flat dish and remove greaseproof paper. Dip a palette knife into water and cut the mousse into ½ inch (1 cm) thick slices, wiping the knife between each cut. Serve with hot, crisp, dry brown toast.

*Note*    If the top of the mousse looks dull, rub the surface with a hot palette knife.

# *H*AM AND
## CHICKEN MOUSSE

*Serves 10–12*

*T*HE texture of this mousse is delicious when made from fresh chicken and ham, and when laboriously pressed through a fine wire sieve after puréeing the meats! However, you may find it more economical to make with left-over meats from Christmas.

*1½ lb (700 g) piece of gammon*
*3–4 lb (1.4–1.8 kg) fresh chicken (or turkey)*

## STOCK FOR COOKING

*1 leek*

*2 carrots*

*1 onion*

*2–3 sticks celery*

*1 clove garlic, cut up*

*½ pint (275 ml) dry white wine*

*Salt*

*12 peppercorns*

*Bouquet garni*

## HAM MOUSSE

*1 pint (570 ml) stock*

*1 sachet (½ oz: 10 g) gelatine crystals*

*1 lb (450 g) ham, cut up*

*2 heaped tsp mild French mustard*

*1 dsp tomato purée*

*Salt and more pepper if necessary*

## CHICKEN MOUSSE

*1 pint (570 ml) stock*

*¾ lb (350 g) chicken breast meat (add enough dark meat to make up)*

*¼ pint (150 ml) bland mayonnaise*

*1 tsp salt*

*1 heaped tsp horseradish cream*

*2–3 tsp lemon juice to taste*

## RED ASPIC JELLY TOPPING

*1 pkt commercial aspic crystals*

*¼ pint (150 ml) port or sherry*

*A touch of cochineal*

Put all the stock ingredients in a large pan. Cover with 2½ pints (1.4 litres) of water. Place the ham and chicken on top, and cook gently for 1 hour. Remove the meat from the stock, and strain this through a sieve lined with kitchen paper. Don't hurry this process. Skin and take all the fat off the ham. Skin and bone the chicken. This will leave you with around ¾–1 lb (350–450 g) ham, and about the same weight of chicken. Make the ham mousse by bringing the strained stock to boiling point. Turn off the heat. Sprinkle the gelatine over and whisk until dissolved. Cool but don't allow to set. Use 1 pint (570 ml) of the stock to make a fine purée of all the other ingredients for the ham mousse in a food processor, then rub this, a little at a time, through a fine sieve. Pour into a wetted 3–4 pint (1.75–2.3 litre) mould or seamless cake tin. Leave to set in the refrigerator. Make the chicken mousse the same way, and pour into the mould on top of the ham layer. Refrigerate.

For a pretty party effect put a ⅓ inch (0.75 cm) layer of red aspic jelly in the bottom of the mould and leave to set before pouring in the ham or chicken mousse. Make up the aspic as directed on the packet, using ¾ pint (400 ml) water and the port or sherry. Cool, then add 1 or 2 drops of cochineal to colour, as liked.

Decorate the mousse as you will with piped stiff mayonnaise, and slices of cucumber, tomato, and hard-boiled eggs. Cut it (it is soft textured) with a palette knife dipped in a jug of boiling water.

# SPINACH AND SALMON 'CUSTARD'

*Serves 6–8*

*T*HE vivid green of this very English dish is most eye-catching. Serve it as you would a terrine.

*1 lb (450 g) young spinach, well washed, de-veined, and patted dry*

*1½ lb (700 g) salmon, skinned and boned*

*3 large eggs, beaten*

*¼ pint (150 ml) single cream*

*1 tsp salt*

*1 level tsp milled pepper*

*½ tsp ground nutmeg*

Preheat the oven to gas mark 4, 350°F (180°C). Butter a lidded terrine or loaf tin and line the base with a piece of buttered paper. Cut half of the salmon into ½ inch (1 cm) cubes. Season lightly. Cut the rest up roughly. With the metal blade fitted to the food processor, drop in the eggs and seasoning. Next add the roughly cut pieces of salmon, and purée finely. Feed in all the spinach and blend everything finely. Scrape the mixture into a bowl. Stir in the cream and the cubed salmon. Pour into the prepared mould and cover with a lid.

Fill a deep container with hot water (it should come to within ½ inch (1 cm) of the rim of the terrine). Fold a piece of newspaper into 4 layers, and place in the bottom. Stand the terrine on this and cook for 1 hour or until the custard is quite set. Cool, then refrigerate overnight. Serve cut into ½ inch (1 cm) slices.

# *P*OTTED SALMON, MARBLED WITH TURBOT AND SCALLOPS

*Serves 8–10*

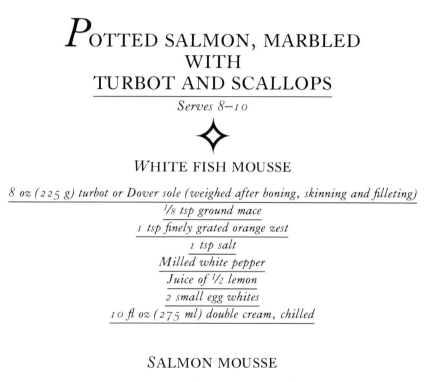

## WHITE FISH MOUSSE

*8 oz (225 g) turbot or Dover sole (weighed after boning, skinning and filleting)*

*⅛ tsp ground mace*

*1 tsp finely grated orange zest*

*1 tsp salt*

*Milled white pepper*

*Juice of ½ lemon*

*2 small egg whites*

*10 fl oz (275 ml) double cream, chilled*

## SALMON MOUSSE

*8 oz (225 g) salmon, weighed as above*

*¼ tsp mixed white pepper*

*1 tsp salt*

*Juice of ½ lemon*

*2 small egg whites*

*10 fl oz (275 ml) double cream, chilled*

*12 queen scallops, fresh or frozen*

*8 oz (225 g) salmon steak*

Preheat the oven to gas mark 4, 350°F (180°C). Have a deepish tin of hot water ready. Butter an oblong terrine approximately 9 × 4 × 4 inches (23 × 10 × 10 cm). Line the base only with a double thickness of buttered greaseproof paper.

Have ready two separate bowls. In one, cut the turbot or sole into bits, toss in the lemon juice and all the seasonings. Beat the egg whites to slacken them a little, and pour over the fish. Cover with plastic film. Chill for an hour or so. Repeat the process with the salmon.

In a food processor, make a fine purée of both mixtures in turn, dribbling in the 10 fluid ounces (275 ml) of chilled cream in one slow but continuous flow. Scrape the purées back into their bowls, and put each into the refrigerator if it's a warm day.

Cut the orange roes from the scallops. Cut into bits, fold into the white fish purée. Poach the scallops in a little milk for 2–3 minutes. Leave to cool, then slice into discs. Reserve. Cut the salmon steak into ½ inch (1 cm) cubes, and fold into the salmon purée.

Put alternate spoonfuls of each purée into the terrine, banging the sides to settle it all in together. Continue until the terrine is filled. Cover with a lid and stand the terrine in a water bath. Cook on the centre shelf of the oven at gas mark 4, 350°F (180°C) for 1¼ hours.

Remove the terrine and take off the lid. Cool for an hour or so. Place a piece of foil-covered board to fit on top of the baked mousse and stand a weight on this. Cool completely: refrigerate.

Turn the mousse out of the terrine by running a hot, wetted palette knife round the sides. Invert the terrine onto a board. Leave to fall out. Remove the dish carefully. Remove the paper and garnish with the scallop discs.

# SAVOURY ROLLED OMELETTE STUFFED WITH COTTAGE CHEESE AND SHRIMPS

*Serves 4–5*

*3 large eggs*
*3 oz (75 g) S.R. flour, sieved*
*Salt and milled white pepper*

## FOR THE FILLING

*12 oz (350 g) cottage cheese*

*¼ pint (150 ml) soured cream*

*1 tsp lemon juice*

*Salt and milled pepper to taste*

*3 hard-boiled eggs, chopped*

*Bunch spring onions, trimmed and chopped*

*6 oz (175 g) (or more) prawns or shrimps (fresh or frozen)*

Preheat the oven to gas mark 6, 400°F (200°C).

Butter and line a 9 × 4 inch (23 × 10 cm) swiss roll tin with silicone paper. Soak a clean tea-towel in cold water and wring out well. Lay it flat on a work surface and place a sheet of silicone paper on top.

Season and whisk the whole eggs until they are ribboning. Dredge over the flour and whisk in. Pour the mixture into the tin and spread evenly into the corners. Place in the oven and bake for 10–12 minutes.

Take out, and invert straightaway carefully onto the paper. Remove the base paper, and roll up the omelette loosely whilst still hot, using the damp tea-towel to help you. Unroll carefully when cool.

Mix the cottage cheese with the soured cream and lemon juice to make the filling. Season well. Gently mix in the remaining ingredients. Spread the filling over the omelette and roll up loosely. Serve cut into broad pieces with extra-creamy mayonnaise.

# *E*NGLAND'S FOUR
# SMOKED FISH MOUSSE

*Serves 10–12*

*T*HIS is a party dish I have created to celebrate our four quality smoked fish – salmon, trout, eel and halibut (or haddock if the latter is not available). You can, of course, just make one of these mousses for a small party.

*8 oz (225 g) smoked salmon*

*8 oz (225 g) smoked trout, weighed after skinning and filleting*

*8 oz (225 g) smoked halibut or haddock, lightly poached*

*4 oz (110 g) smoked eel fillets (see method)*

## FOR EACH MOUSSE

½ pint (275 ml) double cream

¼ pint (150 ml) single cream

8 oz (225 g) smoked fish

1 sachet gelatine crystals dissolved in ½ fl oz (10 ml) whisky,
plus 1½ fl oz (35 ml) boiling water

2 egg whites

Smidgen of cayenne pepper

¼ inch (0.5 cm) tip of a knife-point ground mace

1 tsp lemon juice

A light sprinkling of milled white pepper

## FOR THE LINING

1 lb (450 g) smoked salmon (optional)

Prepare the salmon mousse first. Mix the two creams together and whip to ribbon stage. Make a purée with the fish, egg whites, and the dissolved gelatine. Season lightly with the cayenne, mace, lemon juice and milled pepper. In a large basin cut and mix in the whipped cream thoroughly.

It is well worth the extra luxury of lining the mould with smoked salmon. Prepare a 9 inch (23 cm) mould or terrine approximately 4½ inches (11 cm) deep. Brush all over the inside with olive or soy oil. Cut a piece of greaseproof paper to fit the bottom exactly. If you are lining the mould with smoked salmon slices, allow the side slices to overlap the edge or they will slide down. The edges can then be folded over the top, to act as the top layer.

Pour the smoked salmon mousse into the prepared mould. Leave to set for 30 minutes and place on top a layer of smoked eel fillets, which have been split in half lengthways. Now proceed to the halibut or haddock mousse. Prepare this in exactly the same way as the smoked salmon mousse. Spoon over the smoked eel layer, and level the top. Leave to set for 30 minutes.

Prepare the trout mousse, omitting the ½ fluid ounce (10 ml) of whisky and substituting a fluid ounce (25 ml) of water. Spoon into the mould, cover with the smoked salmon pieces (if used), and leave to chill overnight. It is a softish set.

To unmould, carefully run a warm palette knife round the sides of the mould. Invert onto a platter, and remove the base paper. Dip a knife into a jug of hot water between each cut, and slice into ¼ inch (1.5 cm) slices. Lift each one with a palette knife or cake server.

# POTTED SALMON AND TURKEY WITH HONEY-MINT SAUCE

*Serves 12*

*1–1½ lb (450–700 g) turkey breasts, boned*

*Salt and pepper*

*4 tbsp whisky*

*1 tbsp lemon juice*

*10 oz (275 g) fresh salmon (weighed after skinning and boning),
cut in 1 inch (2.5 cm) pieces*

*2 small eggs*

*½ pint (275 ml) double cream*

*1 level tsp ground mace*

*8 oz (225 g) pistachio nuts, roughly crushed*

*1 lb (450 g) sliced smoked salmon, to line a terrine*

## HONEY-MINT SAUCE

*6 fl oz (175 ml) single cream*

*1 dsp acacia or other flower blossom honey
(heather and clover honey is too strong)*

*2 tbsp raspberry or redcurrant vinegar*

*½ tsp salt*

*Milled white pepper*

*1 tbsp shredded or chopped fresh mint*

Cut the turkey into ½ inch (1 cm) strips, then into ½ inch (1 cm) cubes. Marinate for 2 hours in the whisky and lemon juice. Season well with salt and milled white pepper. Preheat the oven to gas mark 6, 400°F (200°C).

Chill the cream, fresh salmon and eggs. Purée the salmon and eggs in a food processor. Season with salt and the ground mace and pour in the cream in one slow, steady stream, stopping when a stiffish purée is reached. Transfer the purée to a large bowl. Mix in the turkey pieces, the remaining marinade and the pistachio nuts. Line a terrine with the smoked salmon. Brush the bottom and edges with olive oil. Fit a piece of oiled greaseproof paper in the base. Line with the slices of smoked salmon (you might get away with ¾ lb (350 g) if it is thinly cut) and fill with the mixture, spreading well into the corners. Fold over the smoked salmon 'flaps'. Stand the terrine in a tin of hot water. Cover with a lid or buttered foil.

Bake for 1 hour. Cool. Cover with a piece of foil-covered board to fit, and press down with a weight (I use a brick). Refrigerate overnight. Unmould, cut into ⅓ inch (0.75 cm) slices, and serve with a spoonful of the honey-mint sauce.

To prepare this, mix the ingredients together in a basin using a small balloon whisk.

*Note*   In better food shops and delicatessens many new and exciting vinegars are becoming available. However, if these are not in your area, use regular red wine vinegar for the sauce.

# CHEESE AND SHRIMP FRITTERS

*Yields 40–60*

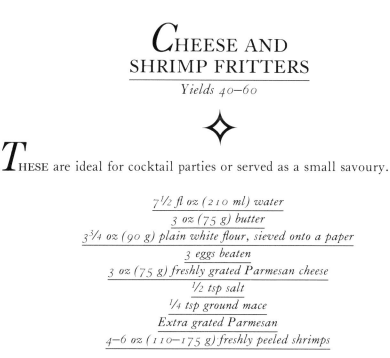

*T*HESE are ideal for cocktail parties or served as a small savoury.

*7½ fl oz (210 ml) water*

*3 oz (75 g) butter*

*3¾ oz (90 g) plain white flour, sieved onto a paper*

*3 eggs beaten*

*3 oz (75 g) freshly grated Parmesan cheese*

*½ tsp salt*

*¼ tsp ground mace*

*Extra grated Parmesan*

*4–6 oz (110–175 g) freshly peeled shrimps*

Put the water and butter into a 4 pint (2.3 litre) pan. Bring to the boil. Season with the salt and mace. Remove from the heat, shoot in the flour at one fell swoop, beating vigorously with a wooden spatula until it is blended and the mixture leaves the sides of the pan in one smooth mass.

Cool for a few minutes, then gradually beat in the eggs and the cheese, holding back a little if the mixture is too soft: it must hold its shape and yet not be too stiff! It should have a good sheen and not look dull. This will take 2–3 minutes.

Line a baking tray with a piece of greaseproof paper. Using a wetted coffee spoon, spoon out rows of the mixture. Press a shrimp into each mound.

Heat a deep fryer to 370°F (190°C). Use clean soy oil for frying. With a palette knife, dipped into the hot fat as necessary, 'knock' or lift 8–10 of the spoonfuls into the fryer. The size of your fryer will depend on how many you can fry at one time. The fritters must have room to swell. As the fritters begin to puff up, increase the temperature of the oil to 400°F (200°C). You will notice as you increase the heat that the fritters will turn themselves over. Cook for 5–6 minutes more until golden-brown (test one to see if it is ready). Lift out with a draining spoon and drain on crumpled paper towels.

Dredge lightly with the extra Parmesan cheese mixed with a speck or two of cayenne pepper. (Use fresh Parmesan only. If you buy it ready-grated in a jar or sachet, it will be gritty due to a substance used to keep the grains apart.)

# WATERCRESS MOUSSES

*Serves 6–8*

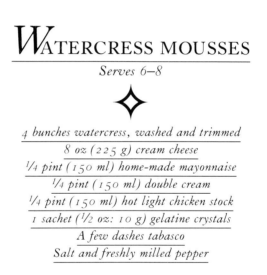

4 *bunches watercress, washed and trimmed*

8 *oz (225 g) cream cheese*

1/4 *pint (150 ml) home-made mayonnaise*

1/4 *pint (150 ml) double cream*

1/4 *pint (150 ml) hot light chicken stock*

1 *sachet (1/2 oz: 10 g) gelatine crystals*

*A few dashes tabasco*

*Salt and freshly milled pepper*

Beat the cheese until smooth. Mix in the mayonnaise. Melt the gelatine in the hot stock and leave to cool. In a food processor, make a purée of the watercress, including the small stalks, using the cooled gelatine as liquid. Add the tabasco and seasoning.

Whip the cream until it *just* holds soft peaks. Cut and mix into this the mayonnaise and cheese mixture, then cut and mix in the watercress purée. Pour into 6–8 individual ramekins, or into a 1½ pint (900 ml) dish or mould. Chill.

# Pasta with Cream and Lemon

*Serves 4*

A TYPE of pasta was eaten in England in medieval times and was known as 'Macraws'. In the eighteenth century they also ate 'Macroni' or 'Macaronies' with rasped Parmesan cheese and cream. Simple and effective. Fresh pasta is available everywhere today. This easy way of preparing thin pasta (linguini, tagliolini) is good with rich spicy dishes.

| |
|---|
| *1 lb (450 g) fresh pasta (linguini)* |
| *¼ pint (150 ml) single cream* |
| *1 clove garlic, crushed (optional)* |
| *1 level tsp grated lemon zest* |
| *Milled pepper* |
| *2 tbsp grated Parmesan cheese* |

Bring a large 8 pint (4.5 litre) non-stick pan full of salted water to the boil. Drop in the pasta and cook for 2–3 minutes only (longer for thicker pasta). Rinse under running hot water. Drain well, banging the sieve or colander to get rid of any water.

Heat the cream with the garlic (if used) in the same pan: add the pasta by degrees, using a pair of tongs to lift and turn it in the cream until it is really hot. Season with milled pepper and the grated lemon zest. Finally sprinkle the Parmesan over, lifting the pasta to mix well in until all is piping hot.

# Chicken Skewers with Apple and Whisky

*Serves 6*

THESE can also be served as an elegant savoury or at cocktail time.

*6 chicken livers soaked overnight in a little milk*

*1 chicken breast, skinned and boned*

*1 Cox's Pippin apple, peeled and cored*

*1 glass whisky*

*2 tbsp olive oil*

*Salt and milled pepper*

*1 tbsp soy sauce (mild)*

*1 level tsp ground mace*

*6 × 4 inch (10 cm) circles of buttered toast*

Mix together the whisky, olive oil, soy sauce, mace and seasoning. Toss the chicken livers, breast and apple in this, and leave for 1 hour, turning the pieces every 15 minutes or so.

Cut the livers in half. Cut the breast in half lengthways, then each half into 6 pieces. Cut the apple in half, then cut each half into 3 wedges, and cut each wedge across.

Oil 12 wooden cocktail sticks, orange sticks, or sate sticks cut in half. Thread two pieces of each item alternately onto each stick. Preheat the grill, and quite fiercely grill the skewers for 1½–2 minutes on each side. Serve on top of the buttered toasts or on a cushion of savoury rice (p. 88).

For cocktail parties, thread only three pieces on each stick.

# SALADS

It never ceases to amaze me that in seventeenth-century England the well-known diarist John Evelyn could write a whole book on salads, their dressings and presentation.✦What a dip into near oblivion the 'sallatt' took over the ensuing centuries!✦Happily, thanks to our healthier approach to eating, the simple salad has now returned to our tables complemented with more exotic dressings than the ubiquitous bottled salad cream. The composite salad takes on a richer life with the marriage of almost any ingredients you may choose.

# CUCUMBER, MINT AND BUTTERMILK SALAD

*Serves 4: side salad*

*1 cucumber, peeled, deseeded and very finely sliced on a machine*

*20 mint leaves, chopped*

*¼ pint (150 ml) buttermilk or plain yoghurt*

*Juice of ½ lemon*

*Salt and white pepper*

*2 tsp sugar*

Make up the dressing by shaking the buttermilk and lemon juice, with the seasoning and sugar, in a screw-topped jar, adding the mint when this is done. Put to chill. Slice the cucumber just before you need it. Toss the slices in the dressing just before serving. Some people like to slice young cucumbers without peeling them. This is a matter of taste.

# LEEK AND GRAPE SALAD

*Serves 4: side salad*

*1 lb (450 g) young, slim leeks, trimmed and washed*

*18 green grapes, skinned, deseeded and halved*

*1 tbsp freshly snipped chives or parsley*

## FOR THE DRESSING

*1 tsp mild French mustard*

*A scant tsp salt*

*Juice of ½ lemon (2 tbsp)*

*1 clove garlic, crushed*

*¼ pint (150 ml) single cream or yoghurt*

In a basin, combine all the dressing ingredients together, using a small balloon whisk.

Use at least half the green part of the leeks and cut them attractively on a strong diagonal slant into ½ inch (1 cm) pieces. Put into a pan of fast-boiling lightly salted water for 2–3 minutes so that they are still crisp.

Drain, and cool under running cold water to retain the leeks' bright green colour. Drain well again for an hour to get rid of excess moisture. Combine the leeks with the grapes and chill well.

Spoon over the dressing just before serving. Sprinkle with the herbs.

# Avocado Pear Salad WITH YOGHURT AND CAPERS

*Serves 4: side salad*

THE tangy dressing is an excellent foil for the buttery texture of the avocado.

*2 ripe avocados*

*Juice of ½ lemon*

*1 tbsp snipped chives and/or parsley*

## FOR THE DRESSING

*1 level tsp dry mustard*

*¼ tsp salt*

*¼ tsp milled black pepper*

*1 tsp caster sugar*

*2 heaped dsp (⅛ pint: 75 ml) natural yoghurt*

*1 heaped tbsp sweet capers, drained*

Mix the ingredients for the dressing in a small basin, adding the capers last. Chill.

Skin the avocados, take out the stones, and cut into slices lengthways. Toss in lemon juice. Serve with the dressing spooned over and sprinkled with the herbs.

# *I*CEBERG LETTUCE SALAD WITH STILTON DRESSING

*Serves 4–6: side salad*

*¹/₂ small Iceberg lettuce, washed and finely shredded*

*1 tbsp snipped chives and/or parsley*

## FOR THE DRESSING

*1 oz (25 g) white part of Stilton cheese*

*1 tbsp oil*

*1 tbsp white wine vinegar*

*2 tbsp yoghurt*

*Salt and milled pepper*

*1 tsp caster sugar*

*¹/₂ tsp mild made mustard*

Press the cheese through a sieve, and combine with the remaining ingredients for the dressing.

Toss the lettuce with the dressing in a large bowl. Transfer to salad plates or a clean salad bowl. Sprinkle with the herbs.

# *P*OTATO AND APPLE SALAD

*Serves 4–6: starter salad*

*³/₄–1 lb (350–450 g) even-sized Pink Fir Apple potatoes, or new potatoes*

*2 Cox's apples, peeled and cored*

*2 tbsp good French dressing*

*Juice of ¹/₂ lemon*

*Page 67 Tartlet of Quails' Eggs with Cottage Cheese and Smoked Salmon*
*Page 68 Spinach and Salmon 'Custard'*

## DRESSING

*2 heaped tbsp good mayonnaise, mixed with 2 tbsp double cream*

*Cold water*

*Milled pepper, plus a good pinch ground mace*

*1/2 clove garlic, crushed*

## TO GARNISH

*1 head white endive, separated and washed*

Boil the potatoes with their skins on in salted water. Drain and peel. Cut into discs whilst still warm and toss in the French dressing until they have absorbed it all. Cool completely. Quarter the apples and slice across to give approximately the same-sized pieces as the potato, and toss in lemon juice to prevent discoloration and add a modest tang.

Mix the ingredients for the dressing together, then carefully turn and fold in the potatoes and apples. Garnish at will with endive leaves.

# *H*ERB GARDEN SALAD

*Serves 4: side salad*

## FOR EACH INDIVIDUAL SALAD SELECT:

*2 inner lettuce leaves*

*2 sorrel leaves*

*1 sprig flat-leafed parsley*

*1 chive flower plus 4–5 stalks of chive*

*2–3 freshly picked applemint or peppermint leaves*

*2–3 tarragon leaves*

*1 spring onion, quartered lengthways*

*1 fennel frond*

*1 frond angelica leaves*

*1 or 2 nasturtium flowers*

*1/2 tsp sweet capers*

*Page 69 Haddock Fish Cakes with Enriched Tartare Sauce    Page 70 New Fried Fish*

## FOR THE DRESSING (FOR 4 SALADS)

*2 fl oz (50 ml) olive or soy oil*

*Juice of 1/2 large lemon*

*1 good tsp flower honey*

*1/4 tsp salt*

*1/4 tsp dry mustard*

Arrange the salad ingredients in a bowl or on 4 separate plates. Shake the dressing ingredients in a screw-topped jar until emulsified. Each guest adds the dressing to their helping, mixing and chopping it with a knife and fork.

# $A$VOCADO WITH REDCURRANT AND ORANGE DRESSING

*Serves 4: starter salad*

*2 avocados*

*Juice of 1 lemon*

*4 inner lettuce leaves, or watercress sprigs*

## FOR THE DRESSING

*8 oz (225 g) redcurrants, frozen or fresh*

*2 tbsp redcurrant vinegar or 1 tbsp red wine vinegar*

*1 level tsp salt*

*2 tsp caster sugar*

*Juice of 1/2 orange*

*1 tbsp rich olive oil*

*A few threads of orange zest for garnish*

Soften the redcurrants in a pan over a low heat with the vinegar, sugar, salt and orange juice, retaining a few whole currants for garnishing. Press the purée through a wire sieve. Cool. Stir in the olive oil.

Halve the avocados, and skin and stone them. Then, using a stainless steel knife, cut into 1/4 inch (0.5 cm) thick slices, lengthwise. Fan each half out attractively. Brush with the lemon juice to prevent discoloration. Arrange on the lettuce leaves or sprigs of watercress and spoon the redcurrant dressing over. Garnish with the threads of orange zest and remaining redcurrants.

# *T*OMATO AND RED ONION SALAD

*Serves 4: side salad*

*2 large even-sized beefsteak tomatoes*
*4 oz (110 g) red onion*
*1 bunch watercress, washed*

## *F*OR THE DRESSING

*2 tbsp olive or soy oil*
*2 tbsp single cream*
*1 tbsp white or red wine vinegar*
*1 level tsp mustard*
*2 tsp caster sugar*
*1 tsp salt*
*1 level tsp milled black pepper*
*1 tbsp freshly chopped parsley*

Cut the stalk and eye out of the tomato. Dip into a pan of boiling water for 10 seconds. Rinse under cold running water, and then peel off the skin. Skin the onion and slice into the thinnest rings possible.

Cut the tomatoes in slices across. Arrange in two rows in a shallow dish, pressing them open into rows with the palm of the hand. Arrange the onion rings over the top, and put the watercress sprigs around.

For once I don't recommend shaking the dressing ingredients in a screw-topped jar, as, if you're too vigorous, the cream may thicken to curdling point. So, mix the dry ingredients with the vinegar. Beat the oil well in. *Mix* in the cream, and dribble the dressing over the salad just before serving.

# Avocado, Prawn and Banana Salad with Salted Pecan Nuts and Yoghurt Dressing

*Serves 4: main course salad*

*T*HIS salad is just right for an impressive summer lunch. It looks attractive and tastes good.

---

*2 ripe avocados, peeled and stoned*

*Juice of 1 lemon*

*1 banana, peeled and diced*

*Salt and milled pepper*

*2 oz (50 g) pecan nuts (or walnuts), roughly crushed*

*8 oz (225 g) peeled prawns (fresh or frozen)*

*1 head Belgian chicory, separated into spears, washed*

*1 oz (25 g) red salmon roe (optional)*

*4 quails' eggs, cooked, shelled, halved — or 2 eggs, quartered*

*1 tbsp freshly snipped chives*

## FOR THE DRESSING

*5 fl oz (150 ml) natural yoghurt*

*1 tbsp lemon juice*

*1 level tsp dry mustard*

*1/2 clove garlic, crushed*

*Salt and milled pepper*

*2–3 dashes tabasco*

---

Cut the avocados and banana into ½ inch (1 cm) cubes and toss in the lemon juice to prevent discoloration. Toast the pecans or walnuts in the oven for 10 minutes at gas mark 5, 375°F (190°C). Salt them lightly. Cool, and roughly crush.

Mix the dressing ingredients together in a large bowl. Mix in the two fruits with the lemon juice, and add the prawns. Season well. Turn the mixture into a serving dish, and push spikes of the chicory attractively round the edge. Scatter over the crushed pecans and the herbs, and garnish with the halved quails' eggs, each topped with a little red caviar. Cover loosely with plastic film, and chill until ready to serve.

# *E*NGLISH WINTER SALAD OR 'CHRISTMAS' SALAD WITH RED WINDSOR DRESSING

*Serves 10–12*

*A* REFRESHING starter on Christmas Day. Make a combination of any (or all!) of the following:

*Radicchio (or finely shredded red cabbage)*

*Peeled, cooked beetroot (not in vinegar), cut into sticks or discs*

*Skinned and seeded tomatoes*

*Carrot sticks, cooked for* 2 *minutes only in chicken stock*

*Red peppers, deseeded, cut into sticks*

*Radishes, cleaned and cut into discs*

*Strawberries*

## *F*OR THE DRESSING

*4 oz (110 g) Red Windsor cheese, crumbled*

*¼ pint (150 ml) olive oil*

*1 tbsp red wine vinegar*

*1 tsp tomato purée*

*¼ pint (150 ml) orange juice*

*1 tsp grated orange rind*

*2 oz (50 g) tin filleted anchovies*

*1 clove garlic (optional)*

*No salt*

*1 level tsp milled pepper*

Make a purée of all the dressing ingredients in a blender. This dressing is not dissimilar in idea, strength and texture to a blue cheese dressing. Don't miss out the anchovies: they're the element of surprise and don't taste fishy. It can be made beforehand and stored in the refrigerator. Toss the salad just before serving — you can serve as one huge salad to accompany a mousse, or as individual side salads. The strawberries are a luxury touch if imported ones are available — if not, use frozen raspberries.

# CHICKEN, AVOCADO AND GRAPEFRUIT SALAD WITH WALNUT DRESSING

*Serves 8: starter salad*

*4 chicken breasts, poached and skinned*

*4 ripe avocados, peeled and tossed in lemon juice*

*4 grapefruits, segmented*

*12 quails' eggs, or 4 hens' eggs, medium to hard boiled*

*4 oz (110 g) walnuts or pecan nuts*

## WALNUT OIL DRESSING

*½ pint (275 ml) walnut oil*

*1 tsp mild French mustard*

*1½ tsp salt*

*1 dsp caster sugar*

*1 tbsp lemon juice or white wine vinegar*

*4 oz (110 g) finely crushed walnuts*

Cut all the salad ingredients into bite-sized chunks or pieces. Arrange at will on a china or glass platter, ready for tossing and dressing at the last moment. Other garnishes, such as radicchio leaves, spears of endive, or tomato segments, can be added as you like.

Prepare the dressing by shaking the walnut oil, French mustard, salt, and sugar with the lemon juice or vinegar in a screw-topped jar. Spoon over the salad, and sprinkle liberally with the crushed nuts. (Or you can use a mild French dressing.) This salad makes an excellent component of a buffet: in which case the quantities given here will serve 10–12 people.

# BROCCOLI
## OMELETTE SALAD

*Serves 6–8: starter or main-course salad*

*1 lb (450 g) broccoli*

*1 pint (570 ml) chicken stock (use a cube)*

*Juice of 1 lemon*

*3 bundles watercress*

*12 eggs*

*Salt, pepper and nutmeg*

*Butter for frying*

### FOR THE DRESSING

*⅓ pint (190 ml) olive oil*

*Juice of 1 large lemon*

*1 level tsp sugar*

*1 level tsp dry mustard*

*1 small clove garlic, crushed*

*Salt and freshly milled pepper*

### TO GARNISH

*1 tbsp each of chopped chives and finely chopped parsley*

Break the broccoli into 1 inch (2.5 cm) bits and boil for 1–2 minutes only in the chicken stock to which you have added the lemon juice. Drain and cool.

Wash and pick over the watercress which must be absolutely fresh. Pick the leaves from 2 of the bundles and put them through a blender with 6 of the eggs. Season well with salt, pepper and nutmeg.

Heat the omelette pan, add a knob of butter but do not let it brown. Make up thin omelettes with the mixture (it should make about 6–8), letting it almost set before turning over with a large palette knife for a mere second: the omelettes must not be hard and tough. Turn on to a work surface and roll them up loosely.

Now make a similar number of omelettes with the remaining eggs, this time omitting the watercress, so that you end up with a mixture of green and yellow toned omelettes. Cut the rolls into ½ inch (1 cm) wide strips, diagonally.

Arrange the broccoli, omelette strips and sprigs of remaining watercress in a large salad bowl. Combine the dressing ingredients and pour it over the salad (it will absorb quite a bit of dressing). Sprinkle over the chives and parsley, and serve immediately.

# ORANGE, AVOCADO AND SMOKED SALMON SALAD

*Serves 4: starter or main-course salad*

*2 avocados, peeled and bathed in lemon juice*
*2 oranges, segmented*
*4 thin slices of Scottish smoked salmon*
*2 spring onions, cut and curled in cold water*
*4 lettuce leaves*

## FOR THE DRESSING

*1 tsp shredded orange zest (called a chiffonnade)*
*⅛ pint (75 ml) rich avocado oil or olive oil*
*1 tbsp orange juice*
*1 tbsp red wine vinegar*
*The tip of a tsp mild French mustard*
*1 tsp muscovado sugar*
*Salt, milled pepper*
*1 level tbsp chopped tarragon, dill or parsley*

## ORANGE CHIVE BUTTER

*2 oz (50 g) soft butter*
*¼ tsp salt*
*The merest sprinkling of ground mace*
*½ tsp finely grated orange zest*
*1 tbsp finely snipped chives*

Shake all the dressing ingredients in a screw-topped jar until well emulsified. Cut the avocados in half, and cut each half in half again. Sprinkle with the dressing to prevent discoloration, wrap a slice of smoked salmon loosely around four of the avocado quarters, and arrange each one on a lettuce leaf. Decorate with the remaining avocado quarters, thinly sliced, the orange segments, and the striplets of spring onion. Splash a little more dressing over the top. Chill a little.

Make the orange chive butter by making a paste of all the ingredients (use a palette knife). Add the chives when all is well mixed. Spread on thin slices of brown bread and serve with the salad.

# *H*OT GREEN BEAN, BACON AND RICE SALAD

## Serves 4

*T*o be served as a cheap and cheerful lunchtime main course, or as a side dish to accompany some rather more substantial dish at a buffet supper.

*½ lb (225 g) prime back bacon, cut into strips*

*14 oz (400 g) tin green (flageolet) beans in brine*

*3 oz (75 g) rice cooked in chicken stock*

*1 pint (570 ml) strong chicken stock, or 2 reconstituted stock cubes*

*2 oz (50 g) onion, finely chopped*

*Small clove garlic, crushed (optional)*

*½ oz (10 g) butter*

### *F*OR THE DRESSING

*2 fl oz (50 ml) olive or soy oil (not corn oil)*

*1 fl oz (25 ml) lemon juice*

*1 level tsp mild French mustard*

*1 level tsp sugar*

*Salt and milled pepper*

Fry the bacon strips, drain and put to keep hot (or re-fry when ready for use). Rinse the beans under cold water and drain well. Cook the rice in the strong chicken stock, stirring to prevent sticking. Drain, retaining liquid for soup at some other time. In a large pan fry the onion in the ½ ounce (10 g) of butter until soft and golden. Add the garlic, if used.

Prepare the dressing, seasoning well with salt and pepper, and shaking together all the ingredients in a screw-topped jar. Pour the dressing into the pan with the onion and bring to the boil. Add the rice and beans and, using a slotted spoon, stir carefully until it is heated right through. Finally mix in the bacon. Spoon the salad into a warm serving dish.

# $M$ICHAEL SMITH'S SPECIAL CRAB SALAD

*Serves 4: main-course salad*

*8 oz (225 g) fresh white crab meat, flaked*

*4 oz (110 g) celery, finely diced*

*4 oz (110 g) cucumber, unpeeled but deseeded and finely diced*

*6 spring onions, finely shredded*

*8 oz (225 g) cottage cheese, drained if necessary*

*4 fl oz (100 ml) soured cream, half whipped*

*2–3 dashes tabasco*

*1 good tsp Colman's horseradish relish*

*1 tbsp lemon juice*

*Salt and milled pepper*

## $O$PTIONAL GARNISHES

*1 head endive or inner lettuce leaves*

*1 tomato, skinned, deseeded and cut into eight petals*

*1 hard-boiled egg, quartered*

*1 spring onion, trimmed and cut lengthways*

*A few cucumber slices*

Combine the cottage cheese, soured cream and horseradish together, seasoning handsomely with salt, pepper and lemon juice to taste. Be sparing with the tabasco, but the dressing should have some kick!

Combine this dressing in a second bowl with the crab meat, celery, cucumber and spring onions, carefully folding them in. The mixture should not be sloppy. Chill well. Transfer to a chilled serving bowl lined with endive leaves or tender lettuce leaves. Garnish at will. Keep the salad refrigerated until ready to serve.

As an added luxury for a summer lunch, serve an extra cracked crab claw and a wedge of lemon separately.

# ORANGE, RED ONION AND WALNUT SALAD

*Serves 4: side salad*

*3 navel or Jaffa oranges*

*1 red onion, peeled*

*2 oz (50 g) shelled walnuts, lightly toasted, cooled and roughly crushed*

*1 tbsp roughly chopped parsley and/or snipped chives*

## FOR THE DRESSING

*½ clove garlic, crushed*

*1 tbsp red wine vinegar*

*3 tbsp rich olive oil*

*1 level tsp mild made mustard*

*1 tsp finely grated orange rind (see method)*

*2 tbsp orange juice (see method)*

*1 tsp caster sugar*

*Salt and milled pepper*

Grate the rind from one of the oranges, and reserve for the dresssing.

Cut the onion into the finest rings possible, separate them and soak in a basin of iced water for 2 hours; drain and pat dry with paper towels. This removes some of their strong flavour (for social reasons only!). Whilst red onions are sweeter and milder than ordinary ones, these can be used in this salad, but I suggest that you put the rings into a basket and dip them in a pan of boiling water for 15 seconds only. Rinse immediately under cold running water and pat dry.

Using a serrated knife, cut the skin off all three oranges, shaving away any white pith you might otherwise miss. Cut each orange into 6–8 rings over a plate so that you catch any flowing juice for use in the dressing.

Arrange the rings, overlapping, in a shallow dish, with the onion rings evenly on top. Lightly toast the shelled walnuts, allow to cool, then roughly crush them. Scatter over the salad with the parsley or chives. Cover with plastic film. Chill well for an hour or so. Make up the dressing by shaking all the ingredients, including the grated orange rind and reserved juice, in a screw-topped jar. Spoon it over the salad just before serving.

# VEGETABLES

✦

*As a nation of market gardeners, our production of vegetables is prolific — but it is the freezer which benefits, almost to surfeit point.*✦*Coupled with this, we still have a tendency to overcook and destroy vegetables by prolonged rapid boiling. Now is the time to kill this habit for once and for all.*✦*Today, with the emphasis on healthier eating, we are beginning to enjoy crisper cooked vegetables, which allows the individual flavour of each to speak for itself. This simpler approach is particularly good when preparing creamy purées of turnips, celeriac or other root vegetables. The complement of one single herb or spice is, to my thinking, enough to enhance the flavour when an exotic approach is wanted.*

# WILTED SPINACH WITH LEMON, NUTMEG AND GARLIC

*Serves 4–6*

2 lb (900 g) fresh spinach, washed, trimmed of stalks

3 oz (75 g) unsalted butter

1 clove garlic, crushed

1 tbsp lemon juice

Salt and milled pepper

1 level tsp ground nutmeg

Melt the butter with the garlic in a large deep pan, without colouring it. Add the spinach, which should have been patted dry. Cover with a lid, then over a medium heat let the spinach 'sink' and wilt. You will need to fork it around in the early stages. As soon as it is hot, season with salt, pepper, nutmeg and lemon juice, mixing it well in. Do not drain.

# SAVOY CABBAGE WITH CARAWAY

*Serves 4–6*

3 lb (1.4 kg) savoy cabbage, finely shredded

1/4 pint (150 ml) soured cream

Salt and milled black pepper

1 tsp caraway seeds

Steam or boil the cabbage (which should be as fine as string) for 2–3 minutes, leaving it somewhat crisp. Drain well.

In a large pan stir the cream and cabbage together over a high heat, sprinkling over the caraway seeds as you toss and turn it. Use a wooden spaghetti fork to facilitate this. Season and serve.

# CREAMED LEEKS WITH GARLIC AND CHIVES

*Serves 4*

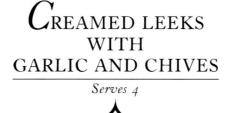

*O*NIONS, garlic, chives and suchlike vegetables come under the heading of 'aromatics'. Here I have used three together to create an elegant dish.

*1 lb (450 g) young leeks, trimmed*
*2 cloves garlic, crushed*
*1 oz (25 g) bunch chives or the green part of young spring onions*
*1 oz (25 g) butter*
*2 tbsp thick cream*
*Salt and milled pepper*

Finely shred the leeks into ⅛ inch (0.25 cm) discs. Wash and drain. Melt the modest amount of butter, without browning it, in a heavy-bottomed pan. Add the leeks, and cover with a lid. Then, over a low heat, toss and stir the leeks until their natural juices start to draw. Simmer them for 2–3 minutes, so that they remain somewhat crisp.

Add the garlic, cream and chives, season lightly and bubble for a minute or two more until the cream has cohered.

# COURGETTES

*Serves 4*

*1 lb (450 g) courgettes*
*Salt*
*Dredge sugar*
*Knob butter*

To cook courgettes so that they're green and crisp, top, tail and wash the courgettes. Slice in *thin* diagonal slices. Bring to the boil a large pan of water to which you have added salt and a dredge of sugar. Tip in the sliced courgettes and leave for 2 minutes with the heat off. Drain, return to the dry pan, add a good knob of butter, toss well and serve immediately.

# $P$AN-BRAISED CELERIAC

*Serves 3–4*

*1 small celeriac root, scrubbed and peeled*

*½ chicken stock cube, dissolved in 4 fl oz (100 ml) boiling water*

*1 glass dry sherry*

*Milled pepper*

*½ oz (10 g) butter*

Have ready a bowl of water to which you have added some lemon juice. Cut the celeriac into ¼ inch (0.5 cm) thick discs (about 5–6). Put into the water to prevent discoloration.

Cook for 2–3 minutes in plenty of boiling salted water. The celeriac should still be crisp. Drain and cool under running cold water. Drain again. Cut into fancy shapes if you have a mind to.

Just before serving, melt the butter in a wide, shallow pan, swirling it round until foaming. Fry the celeriac on both sides until golden. Pour in the stock and sherry; season with the milled pepper. Lower heat and reduce till you have a sticky coating.

# $C$AULIFLOWER CHEESE

*Serves 4*

$I$ TACKLED the task of restyling this dish to fit the mood and taste of the 1980s by referring back, as I very often do, to the methods of the 1700s. I think that this is one of the great discoveries of the book.

*1 good white cauliflower, broken into 1 inch long (2.5 cm) florets*

*¼ pint (150 ml) single cream*

*½ clove garlic, crushed*

*1 heaped tbsp freshly grated Parmesan cheese*

*Juice of ½ lemon*

*¼ tsp ground mace*

*More salt if required*

The secret of success with this dish is to mix the cheese with the garlic, mace and cream and allow it to stand for 2 hours.

Drop the cauliflower florets into boiling, salted water to which you have added the juice of half a lemon, and cook for 2–3 minutes. The cauliflower should remain crisp. Drain well. Add the cauliflower to the pan containing the cream mixture and toss and bubble over a medium to high heat until each floret is well coated, and all is well blended.

*Note* The cauliflower can be cooked in advance, rinsed under cold running water to cool completely, and then drained well. Reheat with the cream mixture over a low heat, tossing and stirring well until piping hot.

# $G$LAZED CARROT STICKS WITH GINGER AND ORANGE

*Serves 8*

*8 large new carrots or 4 small–medium older ones*

*½ pint (275 ml) orange juice*

*¾ chicken stock cube*

*1 level tsp ground ginger*

*¼ tsp salt*

*1 oz (25 g) unsalted butter*

*½ clove garlic, uncut*

Peel the carrots, trimming the sides. Cut into ½ inch (1 cm) slices, then into ¼ inch (0.5 cm) sticks. Add the stock cube and ground ginger to the orange juice, and bring to the boil. Cook the carrots in this for 3–4 minutes –

they should remain somewhat crisp. Drain, retaining the liquid. Reduce this, with the garlic added, by boiling rapidly until viscous.

Remove the garlic clove, then add the butter and the cooked carrot sticks, tossing around over the heat until hot and coated with the sauce.

# SAVOURY RICE

*Serves 4*

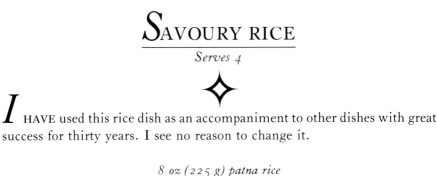

*I* HAVE used this rice dish as an accompaniment to other dishes with great success for thirty years. I see no reason to change it.

*8 oz (225 g) patna rice*

*20 fl oz (550 ml) chicken stock*

*4 rashers bacon, finely diced*

*1 onion, finely chopped*

*2 cloves garlic, finely chopped or crushed*

*4 oz (110 g) mushrooms, finely chopped*

*2 sticks celery, diced*

*Salt and milled pepper*

## TO FINISH THE RICE

*3 oz (75 g) freshly grated Parmesan cheese (or 'dry' Gruyère)*

*2 oz (50 g) butter*

*1 tbsp thick cream*

*1 tbsp freshly chopped parsley*

Preheat the oven to gas mark 7, 425°F (220°C). Fry the bacon until almost crisp. Transfer to an ovenproof pot. Fry the onion and celery in the bacon fat until soft, adding the garlic as you finish. Add the mushrooms and fry for a minute or two. Add the rice and fry again.

Transfer everything to the ovenproof pot. Bring the stock to the boil, pour over the rice mixture and stir well, seasoning with salt and pepper to taste. Cook in the oven for 20 minutes, until all the liquid is absorbed. Just before serving, stir in the butter, cheese and cream with a fork. Garnish with the chopped parsley.

# BAKED BELGIAN ENDIVE WITH PEARS AND CREAM CHEESE

*Serves 6*

4 small heads endive

4 ripe pears

Juice of 1 large lemon

1 tbsp caster sugar

1/2 pint (275 ml) double cream

Salt and milled pepper

4 oz (110 g) cottage cheese

Preheat the oven to gas mark 7, 425°F (220°C).

Blanch the endive for 3–4 minutes in boiling water to which you have added a little lemon juice and sugar. Remove from the pan, and drain well, then cut in quarters lengthways. Peel, core and quarter the pears and toss them in lemon juice.

Now arrange the endive and pear quarters alternately to make a single layer in a round, shallow ovenproof dish. Season with salt and pepper. Pour the cream over and spread the cheese evenly across the surface. Season again lightly with salt and pepper and about 1 teaspoon of caster sugar. Bake at gas mark 7, 425°F (220°C) for 20 minutes or until hot, brown and bubbly.

# POTATO AND MUSHROOM RAMEKINS

*Serves 4*

6 oz (175 g) white-cap mushrooms

6 even-sized waxy new potatoes

1/4 pint (150 ml) double cream

Salt, pepper and a smidgen of nutmeg

2 oz (50 g) fresh breadcrumbs, toasted in the oven

Wipe the mushrooms clean. Quarter them. Scrape or peel the potatoes, cut into small cubes, and cover with cold water. Simmer the mushrooms in the cream for 2 minutes. Strain, retaining the liquor.

Cook the potato cubes in the liquor until just tender but not collapsed. Stir them from time to time as the cream reduces. Add the mushrooms to the pan, mixing well. Season well with salt, pepper and nutmeg. Pour into individual ramekins and scatter the toasted breadcrumbs over.

These can be made in advance. To serve, just reheat in the oven at gas mark 6, 400°F (200 °C) for 10 minutes.

# $P$URÉES

$A$ SUCCESSFULLY presented vegetable purée is unbelievably delicious, and shows each vegetable off in a unique and elegant way. A wet, sloppy purée is a bore and ought never to be served. Just how to get a good dry purée to which cream will be added can present a problem. Here's how I make mine.

Allow 4 ounces (110 g) unpeeled roots (carrots, turnips, etc.) per serving. Take 2 pounds (900 g) of peeled roots of even size, if they're small, or cut into equal-sized pieces if using larger roots. (Old, marked and woody vegetables should not be used.) Boil them in chicken stock (preferably) or lightly salted water at a slow roll, for 10–15 minutes, or until quite tender. (Crisply cooked root vegetables will give a grainy purée.)

Drain them and pass through a mouli directly into a basin lined with muslin or a fine linen kitchen towel. Allow the purée to cool and drain well, twisting the muslin to help this process. You will be amazed at the amount of liquid which is squeezed out – upwards of ½ pint (275 ml)! This is to be replaced by the cream, thus restoring a good consistency, and enriching the purée without making it too watery.

In a non-stick pan melt 2 ounces (50 g) unsalted butter in ¼ pint (150 ml) of single cream. Sprinkle in a generous dredge or two of finely grated nutmeg, 1 teaspoon caster sugar and a possible 2 teaspoons of lemon juice (about ½ teaspoonful to begin with), adding more later if you like it more lemony.

Lower the heat and add the cool purée, a spoonful at a time, stirring well all the time with a wooden spatula until the purée is steaming hot. You will probably need to add more cream as you go along: just how much will depend on the amount of liquid you originally extracted and on the finished consistency you prefer. Pile into a warmed tureen for serving.

A quicker way to make this purée would be to dry the drained vegetable over a low heat in the pan before puréeing in a blender or other food processor, adding the hot cream, butter and seasoning as you go along.

# CELERIAC PURÉE

*Serves 4–6*

| |
|---|
| *1½ lb (700 g) celeriac* |
| *Juice of ½ lemon* |
| *2 oz (50 g) butter* |
| *⅛ pint (75 ml) double cream* |
| *Salt, milled white pepper* |

Wash and peel the celeriac. Cut into even-sized pieces and put immediately into water with the lemon juice added to prevent discoloration. Cook in lightly salted water until tender. Drain, returning the celeriac to the pan to dry out the excess moisture over a lower heat. Stir whilst doing this.

Make a fine purée by passing the vegetables through a mouli, and then through a fine-meshed sieve. Heat the cream and butter in a non-stick pan, stir in the purée to heat through. Season nicely.

# MASHED POTATOES

*Serves 6*

| |
|---|
| *1½ lb (700 g) floury potatoes* |
| *¼ pint (150 ml) hot milk* |
| *1 oz (25 g) butter* |
| *A dredge of nutmeg* |

Boil or steam the potatoes in the usual way. If boiled, drain, return them to the pan, and over a low heat dry out any excess moisture. Press through a potato ricer. Beat in the modest amount of butter and milk: the mixture should be fairly firm if you are combining it with choux pastry (see p. 217). Otherwise add ¼ pint (150 ml) single cream, heated with 3 ounces (75 g) good butter and a ¼ teaspoon ground nutmeg to make a creamier consistency.

*Note:* Combined with choux pastry, this can be used as a topping to Shepherd's Pie (p. 145), or as a mixture for scones (p. 45).

# FISH

◇

*Considering that we are an island surrounded by fish-laden seas, we make precious little use of our catch, much of it going abroad for others to consume. Happily, there are now signs of improvement. In this section I have included many new and exciting ideas for using fish, but — and I think perhaps more importantly — I have taken those two British institutions, fried fish and fish cakes, and given them an exciting face-lift straight into the 1990s, without losing their national character. My new batter is deliciously light and crispy, and I have done nothing to the three main ingredients for fish cakes — fish, potatoes and eggs — other than work with them in a 'fresh raw' rather than a 'stale left-over' state. The results are magical!*

# NEW FRIED FISH

*Serves 4*

To ensure a light, crisp batter acceptable to the new thinking, I have gone directly to Japan and used a tempura batter. The fish is English!

*4–6 oz (110–175 g) halibut, cut into 4 pieces*
*4–6 oz (110–175 g) turbot, cut into 4 pieces*
*2 fillets Dover sole, cut in half diagonally*
*4 fillets haddock, skinned and cut into 4 pieces*

## MARINADE

*2 tbsp soy oil*
*1 tbsp lemon juice*
*Salt and milled pepper*
*1 small clove garlic, crushed*

## BATTER

*4 oz (110 g) plain white flour, sieved*
*1½ oz (40 g) rice flour or cornflour*
*1½ oz (40 g) arrowroot*
*1 egg, separated*
*½ pint (275 ml) water*
*1 level tsp salt*

Put the 16 pieces of fish in a glass bowl with the marinade. Leave for 30 minutes.

Sieve all the dry ingredients together into a bowl and make a well in the middle. Mix the egg yolk with the water, incorporate into the flour and beat to a smooth batter. Beat the egg white until stiff, then cut and fold it into the mixture.

Have your deep fryer filled ⅓ full with soy oil. Heat the oil, and test the temperature by dropping a spoonful of the batter into it: it should float to the surface and sizzle straightaway. Dip each piece of fish in the batter, shake away any surplus (this is a very thin light coating). Fry in small batches (so as not to lower the temperature of the oil) until golden and crisp. Drain on kitchen paper. Serve immediately with lemon wedges and/or a sauce of your choice.

If you need to keep the fish hot, stand a metal baking sheet over a pan of simmering water and put the fish on this, or in the oven with the door open so that the fish remains crisp.

# *H*ADDOCK FISH CAKES WITH ENRICHED TARTARE SAUCE

*Serves 5–6*

*A*LL the elements of the traditional fish cake are brought together here, but the ingredients are all raw: the result is a remarkable renaissance for this favourite dish. You can serve them with lemon wedges for breakfast or, accompanied by my new enriched tartare sauce, they will grace the brunch table or act as a dinner-time starter.

*1 lb (450 g) fresh haddock, filleted, skinned and boned*

*2 beaten eggs*

*8 oz (225 g) raw potato, peeled and cubed into cold water*

*2 slices white bread, crustless, cut into small squares*

*¹/₈ pint (75 ml) single cream*

*Salt and milled pepper*

*Clarified butter or soy oil for frying*

## FOR THE SAUCE

*¹/₂ pint (275 ml) home-made mayonnaise*

*A little lemon juice or water*

*1–2 dashes tabasco*

*1 hard-boiled egg, shelled and halved*

*4–5 American cocktail gherkins, finely chopped*

*1 tbsp chives, finely snipped (or parsley or other green herb)*

*1 oz (25 g) prawns, chopped*

*3–4 anchovy fillets, separated and diced*

Make a fine purée of all the ingredients in a food processor, adding the cream last of all so that it isn't overworked. For an extra fine texture, rub the mixture through a fine sieve.

The mixture should be softish. Have ready a jug of cold water and a dessertspoon (for large cakes) or a teaspoon (for small ones). Scoop out spoonfuls on to a wetted work surface, dipping the spoon in water each time. Using a wetted knife or palette knife, level and shape the cakes which should be about ½ inch (1 cm) thick.

In a skillet or frying pan heat 2–3 tablespoons of clarified butter or soy oil to smoking point. Lift and slide the cakes into the smoking oil in batches of 5 or 6. Turn them after ½ minute, when a golden crust will have formed. Lower the heat and cook and turn them for 3–4 minutes. Drain on kitchen paper towels. Add a little more oil or butter when required.

For added luxury, a large peeled 'crevette' or American shrimp tail can be pressed into the mixture, and half a clove of crushed garlic plus 2 tablespoons of finely chopped fresh parsley can also be added. The cakes are delicious served cold, sliced and dressed with oil and vinegar or mayonnaise, or with my special tartare sauce. To prepare this, chop the hard-boiled egg white, and sieve the yolk onto a saucer. Mix the mayonnaise to the texture of double cream with a little lemon juice or water. Add the tabasco. Stir in the sieved yolk, retaining a spoonful to sprinkle over as a garnish if you like, and mix in the remaining ingredients. Cover with plastic film, and chill ready for use.

# *P*AN-FRIED HALIBUT WITH RED PEPPERS, GINGER AND ORANGE

*Serves 4*

*2 lb (900 g) halibut steak or fillets*

*1 piece stem ginger, cut into discs or shredded*

*1 red pepper, deseeded and cut into matchsticks*

*1 large orange, knife-peeled and segmented*

*2 oz (50 g) butter for frying*

*1 double whisky*

*Juice of ½ orange*

Have your fishmonger skin and fillet the halibut into its natural four segments. Heat a good ounce (25 g) of butter in a non-stick frying pan, swirling it round to ensure even heating. When hot, fry the halibut pieces for 2–3 minutes on each side. Season nicely. Transfer to a warm serving dish.

Add a further ounce (25 g) of butter to the pan and let it foam and go almondy. Pour in the whisky and orange juice. Allow this to bubble, then quickly cook the pepper matchsticks in this sauce until soft. Add the stem ginger. Spoon over the fish, and garnish with orange segments.

# $F$ILLETS OF DOVER SOLE WITH PRAWNS, RADICCHIO AND MARTINI SAUCE

*Serves 2*

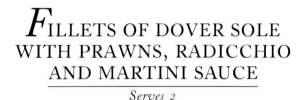

$H$ERE is a delicious way of using this 'red lettuce' that is now readily available in our shops.

*2 large single or 2 small double fillets of Dover sole, skinned*
*1 small head radicchio*
*8 Mediterranean prawns, frozen, defrosted and shelled. Retain débris*
*1 pint (570 ml) fish stock (see p. 24)*
*¼ pint (150 ml) dry martini*
*¼ pint (150 ml) single cream*
*Salt and milled pepper*

Take ½ pint (275 ml) of the fish stock, add to it the wine, and reduce to ¼ pint (150 ml) by boiling rapidly. Add the débris from the prawns and the cream and simmer for 15 minutes. Season lightly. Strain into a small basin, put on one side.

With a wetted rolling pin or milk bottle, very gently pat the fillets of sole until you just feel the fibres resist. Lay them on a plate, good side down. Season lightly. Lay over enough radicchio leaves to cover. Place 2 prawns on each and roll up. Secure with 2 cocktail sticks.

Place the stuffed fillets in a small, shallow pan just large enough to contain them and pour over the remaining fish stock. Cover with a circle of buttered greaseproof paper and a lid.

Bring to the boil and cook gently for 4–5 minutes (longer if you like fish well cooked). Place the remaining prawns on top of the paper to heat through for 2 minutes. Remove the paper. Take out the fillets with a draining spoon, place in a serving dish, garnish with the prawns. Bring the small amount of rich sauce to the boil. Pour over the fish and serve.


# *F*ILLETS OF
## RAINBOW TROUT WITH CRANBERRY SAUCE

*Serves 2*

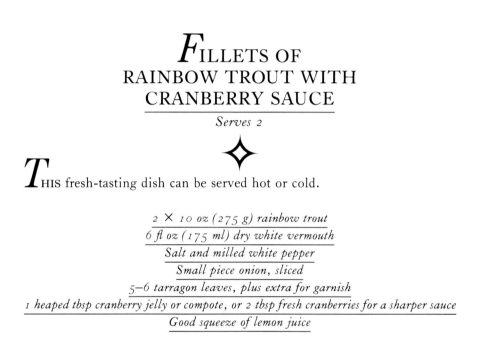

*T*HIS fresh-tasting dish can be served hot or cold.

*2 × 10 oz (275 g) rainbow trout*
*6 fl oz (175 ml) dry white vermouth*
*Salt and milled white pepper*
*Small piece onion, sliced*
*5–6 tarragon leaves, plus extra for garnish*
*1 heaped tbsp cranberry jelly or compote, or 2 tbsp fresh cranberries for a sharper sauce*
*Good squeeze of lemon juice*

Cut off the heads and tails of the trout. Wash the fish well. Place them side by side in a shallow sauté pan and pour over the vermouth. Season lightly. Scatter over the pieces of onion and the tarragon. Cover with a circle of buttered paper, then with a lid. Bring to the boil and simmer for 3–4 minutes. Remove the trout, leave to cool a little, then remove the skin. Reduce the liquid in the pan by half by boiling rapidly, uncovered. Add the cranberry jelly or fresh cranberries. Simmer until incorporated, or the fresh cranberries are pulped. Sieve finely. Add the lemon juice and check the seasoning. Cover with plastic film and leave to cool. When the trout are cold, fillet them by cutting down the centre back and lifting away the two top fillets. Trim off any untidy bits. Invert the top fillets onto a plate or dish, then gently lift out the backbone and invert the two bottom fillets on top of those already in the dish. Pour around a little of the sauce. Garnish with the extra blanched tarragon leaves, or a little freshly chopped tarragon.

# *P*AN-FRIED TROUT WITH TWO HERBS

*Serves 4*

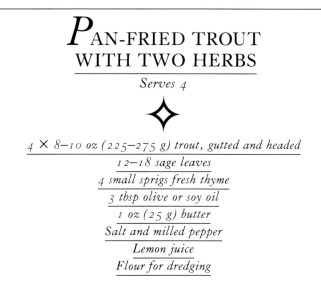

4 × 8–10 oz (225–275 g) trout, gutted and headed
12–18 sage leaves
4 small sprigs fresh thyme
3 tbsp olive or soy oil
1 oz (25 g) butter
Salt and milled pepper
Lemon juice
Flour for dredging

Season the inside of each trout with salt, pepper and a good squeeze of lemon juice. Fill with the sage leaves and thyme sprigs. Dredge the trout lightly with seasoned flour on both sides.

Heat the oil and butter in a large frying pan, swirl around until the butter is evenly melted and beginning to brown slightly. Fry the trout over a medium to high heat for 10 minutes, turning them about every 2 minutes. The trout are cooked when the flesh gives when pressed gently in the thickest part with the tip of a forefinger. Drain, and serve with a spoonful of chive butter (see pp. 109–10).

# *P*OACHED SALMON WITH SHERRY CREAM SAUCE

*Serves 4*

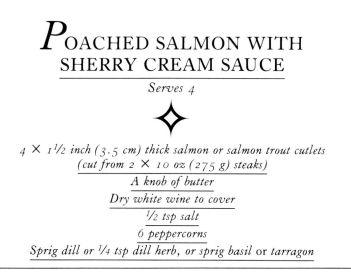

4 × 1½ inch (3.5 cm) thick salmon or salmon trout cutlets
(cut from 2 × 10 oz (275 g) steaks)
A knob of butter
Dry white wine to cover
½ tsp salt
6 peppercorns
Sprig dill or ¼ tsp dill herb, or sprig basil or tarragon

## SHERRY CREAM SAUCE

*4 fl oz (100 ml) cooking stock*
*4 fl oz (100 ml) Amontillado sherry*
*8 fl oz (225 ml) double cream*
*A little salt*
*Freshly milled white pepper*
*1 tbsp freshly chopped basil, tarragon or dill*

Choose a shallow pan which is just large enough to contain the salmon cutlets. Butter it and arrange the salmon in it. Pour over enough dry white wine to just cover. Add the herbs and seasonings. Bring to the boil, reduce heat and simmer with a lid on (or cover with foil) for 10 minutes.

Remove the fish, take off the skin, and arrange on a warm serving dish.

Add the sherry to the stock in which you have cooked the salmon cutlets, and reduce to 4 fluid ounces (100 ml) by boiling rapidly in an enamel or stainless steel pan. Add the cream and reduce again to 10 fluid ounces (275 ml). Season delicately. Add the freshly chopped herbs just before serving. If the cream shows signs of 'oiling', add a modicum of water and whisk it in. Pour over the salmon cutlets and serve.

# $B$AKED OYSTERS WITH CREAM AND PARMESAN

*2 large oysters per serving*
*2 dashes tabasco per serving*
*2–3 drops lemon juice*
*1 tsp double cream per serving*
*Smidgen of salt*
*Mere screw of milled pepper*
*Light dredging of freshly grated Parmesan cheese*
*Oyster liquor (juice)*

Preheat the oven to gas mark 7, 425°F (220°C).

Open the oysters over a bowl to catch the juice. Arrange each oyster on the deep half of the shell. Season with the tabasco, salt, pepper and lemon juice. In a cup mix the oyster juice with the cream. Spoon over each oyster, dredge very lightly with the Parmesan. Stand them on a small baking tray or in an ovenproof dish. Bake in the oven until just bubbling and a light golden-brown. Eat immediately.

# *F*RICASSEE OF FISH IN MUSTARD SAUCE

*Serves 4*

*4 large scallops, cut in half across, including coral*

*16 fresh mussels, well scrubbed*

*1½ lb (700 g) monkfish (or turbot or Dover sole),
to yield 14–16 oz (400-450 g) when filleted*

*½ oz (10 g) butter*

*1 tbsp good olive oil*

*2 tbsp whisky*

## FOR THE SAUCE

*1 pint (570 ml) fish stock (see p. 24)*

*½ pint (275 ml) medium dry white wine*

*½ pint (275 ml) double cream*

*1 dsp mild French mustard (or to taste)*

*Salt and pepper*

*Squeeze of lemon juice*

Have your fishmonger fillet and skin the monkfish. There should be 2 long fillets. Carefully trim off any fine membrane-like skin. Cut the fish into 'roundels' or sticks about 1 inch (2.5 cm) thick.

Make the sauce by reducing the wine to ⅓ pint (190 ml) by boiling rapidly in a stainless steel or enamel pan. Add the stock and boil rapidly again to reduce to ¼ pint (150 ml). (This could take about 30 minutes.) Add the cream and reduce again, this time to ½ pint (275 ml). Whisk in the mustard. Season lightly with salt and pepper and a squeeze of lemon juice. Keep hot in a basin over simmering water.

Heat the butter and oil in a large (10–12 inch: 25.5–30.5 cm) frying pan. Swirl round until 'hazing' and hot. Quickly fry the monkfish, moving it around until lightly coloured. This need take only 2 minutes. Flame with 2 tablespoons of whisky and transfer to a warm serving dish. Reduce the pan juices to a dribble and whisk into the hot sauce in the basin.

Meanwhile (or beforehand if you prefer) bring ½ inch (1 cm) of lightly salted water to the boil in a large pan. Toss in the washed mussels and the scallops. Cover with a lid and boil rapidly for 1½ minutes. The mussels will be open and the scallops lightly cooked. Add to the monkfish and arrange individual portions on separate plates. Dribble the sauce over and serve.

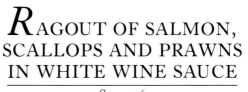

# *R*AGOUT OF SALMON, SCALLOPS AND PRAWNS IN WHITE WINE SAUCE

*Serves 6*

*2 lb (900 g) piece of middle-cut farmed salmon*

*8 scallops*

*6 oz (175 g) fresh peeled prawns*

*6 hard-boiled eggs, quartered*

## POACHING LIQUID

*Cold water to cover*

*½ pint (275 ml) dry white wine*

*1 onion, sliced*

*1 carrot, cleaned and sliced*

*1 bouquet garni sachet*

*Salt and 12 peppercorns*

## FOR THE SAUCE

*¼ pint (150 ml) salmon stock (see method)*

*¾ pint (400 ml) double cream*

*4 oz (110 g) white button mushrooms, quartered*

*¼ pint (150 ml) dry white wine*

*Page 103 Leek and Grape Salad*
*Page 104 Roast Stuffed Double Chicken Breast with Glazed Chestnuts*

Cook the salmon in the following manner. Choose a pan just large enough to contain the fish and just cover with the cold water. Add the wine, onion, carrot, bouquet garni, peppercorns, and a little salt. Bring to the boil, simmer for 10 minutes, then turn off the heat, adding the scallops as you do so. Leave to cool in the liquid. When cooled, remove from the liquid and skin, bone and flake the fish. Cut the scallops in half horizontally. All this can be done beforehand and put on one side.

Make the sauce by straining 1 pint (570 ml) of the cooking liquor from the salmon into a stainless steel or enamel pan. Reduce to ¼ pint (150 ml) by boiling rapidly. Add the cream, white wine and mushrooms. Boil for 5 minutes. Add the flaked salmon and the scallops, lower the heat and mix in, turning everything gently with a large slotted spoon. Add the eggs and prawns 2 minutes before serving, allowing just enough time for them to heat through. Sprinkle with chopped parsley or chervil.

# $R$ICH FISH PASTY

*Serves 6–8*

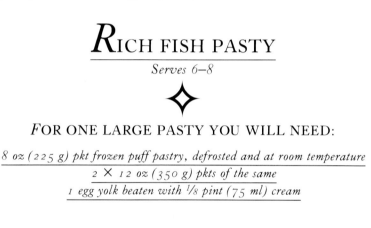

## FOR ONE LARGE PASTY YOU WILL NEED:

*8 oz (225 g) pkt frozen puff pastry, defrosted and at room temperature*

*2 × 12 oz (350 g) pkts of the same*

*1 egg yolk beaten with ⅛ pint (75 ml) cream*

## FOR THE FILLING

*8 oz (225 g) long grain rice, cooked, rinsed and cooled*

*1½ lb (700 g) farm or wild salmon (tail piece)*

*1½ lb (700 g) Dover sole fillets (any white firm-fleshed fish will do, such as turbot, monkfish, halibut, etc.)*

*8 oz (225 g) button mushrooms, quartered*

*½ pint (275 ml) double cream*

*1 level tsp mild French mustard*

*Salt and milled pepper*

*1 fl oz (25 ml) brandy*

*1 oz (25 g) butter*

*2 tbsp freshly chopped flat-leafed parsley*

*½ teacup fish or chicken stock*

Cut both the fish into ½ inch (1 cm) cubes. Quarter the mushrooms. Melt the butter in a large frying pan: when foaming, toss in the mushrooms and fry over a brisk heat. Pour over the brandy and allow to ignite. Quench the flames by pouring over the cream. Stir in the mustard. Season well and allow to bubble for 2–3 minutes. Cool completely.

Boil the rice in fish or chicken stock for 20 minutes: drain and cool. Place the cubed fish in a large bowl and mix in all the other ingredients. Season with salt and milled pepper. The mixture should be moist but hold its shape, so reserve some of the mushroom and fish stock until you see how things are. The filling can be made 2 days in advance, kept covered and refrigerated (not frozen). Assemble the pasty the day before. If it is to be eaten cold, it should be baked on the morning of the party and allowed to cool. Don't refrigerate once cooked: this spoils the pastry.

Preheat the oven to gas mark 6, 400°F (200°C). Invert a swiss roll tin 14 × 9 inches (35.5 × 23 cm), or a large baking sheet of a similar size. Butter it lightly – this will help you remove the pasty when it is baked. Roll out one of the 12 oz (350 g) packets of pastry to approximately the same size as the base tin. Place it on the tin and brush all over with the egg mixture.

Roll out the smaller amount of pastry to approximately 9 × 5 inches (23 × 12.5 cm). Cut a paper template to make a fish shape, and use this to cut a pastry fish. Cut out a small ring ½ inch (1 cm) in diameter for the eye. Brush all over with the egg mixture. Use a teaspoon to make rows of indentations to look like fish scales.

Pile the fish mixture onto the base pastry, then roll out the second 12 oz (350 g) packet of pastry to the same size and lay on top. Press the edges together well. Turn them up and over, pinching to form a firm edge. Stick the fish shape with the eye on top. Cut two steam holes, using an apple corer. Brush all over with the egg mixture. Bake in the preheated oven for 1¼ hours. Serve hot with plenty of hollandaise sauce, or cold with a creamy mayonnaise.

# *E*LEGANT CRAB FISH CAKES ON MINI MUFFINS

*Yields 20–24*

*T*HESE are small enough to be served with cocktails; or you can serve 2 or 3 as a starter, or as a surprise savoury at the end of a dinner menu.

8 oz (225 g) dark crab meat
5 oz (150 g) monkfish, salmon or halibut
1 level tsp salt
1 egg
2 tbsp double cream
1 tsp tomato purée
1 tsp mild sweet paprika
1 tbsp freshly chopped tarragon, chives or parsley (optional version)
Milled pepper
2 oz (50 g) butter and oil for frying

## MINI MUFFINS

2 eggs, beaten, plus 1 egg yolk
1 level tsp salt
2 heaped tbsp S.R. flour
Juice of ½ lemon
Milled pepper

## TOMATO BUTTER

6 oz (175 g) butter, softened
3 tsp tomato purée
Pinch of dry mustard
2 tsp lemon juice

Prepare the muffins first. Make a batter with the above ingredients by pouring the beaten egg gradually into the seasoned flour. Beat in the lemon juice. Brush a hot griddle or non-stick frying pan with a little butter. Drop teaspoons of the batter onto this, 6 at a time, turning the muffins as soon as they are set, and letting them *just* brown on the reverse side, so they are still somewhat soft. Keep them warm, wrapped in a clean towel, in a low oven, gas mark ½, 250°F (130°C) or on a hotplate.

Have all the ingredients for the crab cakes well chilled. In a blender or food processor make a fine purée of the crab meat, fish, egg and seasoning. Add the tomato purée and paprika, and herbs if used, and continue blending. Transfer the mixture to a basin and beat in the chilled cream.

Heat ⅛ inch (0.25 cm) of oil in a frying pan with 2 ounces (50 g) of butter. Swirl round to ensure the butter is evenly but lightly browned. Using a wetted teaspoon, scoop up rounded spoonfuls of the mixture and fry for a minute or so on each side. Transfer to a warm dish. Serve on top of a warm muffin, buttered lightly with tomato butter, made by combining all the ingredients to a smooth paste. It should be used soft. Freeze any left over for future use on top of grilled fish, chicken or chops.

# $L$IGHT SALMON KEDGEREE

*Serves 4*

6 oz (175 g) piece salmon or salmon trout

6 oz (175 g) long grain rice

16 tiny button mushrooms (or 4 larger ones, quartered)

12 quails' eggs boiled for 4 minutes, cooled, shelled and halved

1 oz (25 g) unsalted butter

1/3 pint (190 ml) single cream mixed with 2 egg yolks

A tip of a tsp each of mild curry powder and ground mace

Milled pepper and more salt if necessary

1 tbsp roughly chopped flat-leafed parsley

## $F$OR THE POACHING LIQUID

1/4 pint (150 ml) dry white wine

1 small bouquet of herbs (or 1 sachet)

1 carrot, peeled and roughly diced

1 small onion, peeled and roughly chopped

3/4 pint (400 ml) cold water

1 tsp white peppercorns

1 level tsp salt

Juice of 1/2 lemon

Bring the ingredients for the poaching liquid slowly to the boil: simmer for 5 minutes. Put in the piece of salmon and simmer for 10 minutes. Remove the fish, skin and bone it, and then carefully flake the flesh. Put on one side covered with foil.

Strain the poaching liquid into a clean pan. Bring to the boil and cook the rice in this for 12 minutes (or longer if you prefer rice soft). Drain, and use the liquor to cook the mushrooms for 1 minute; drain these and keep them warm.

Melt the butter in a shallow pan, add the curry and mace, stir in the rice, season with 6–8 turns of the pepper mill and extra salt if necessary; incorporate the flaked salmon. Finally, pour over the egg and cream mixture, and fold and stir everything together over a low heat until it is hot but not curdled. Divide between 4 warm plates, garnish with the quails' eggs, cooked mushrooms and a sprinkling of parsley.

# SHELLFISH WITH QUAILS' EGGS IN WHITE WINE JELLY

*Serves 4–6*

ONCE our English mastercooks had discovered how to clarify liquids, they went berserk making transparent 'soops' (sic), fish ponds, fishes in jelly and many other dishes to excite their guests. Here I have devised a simple, elegant, but quite exotic summer main dish (it may also be served as a starter).

*8 frozen crayfish*
*4 oz (110 g) fresh peeled prawns or shrimps*
*2 lobster tails (frozen)*
*1 small bunch chives, snipped*
*8 quails' eggs, fresh, bottled or tinned*

## WHITE WINE JELLY

*1 pkt Reiber aspic jelly powder, or other commercial brand*
*1 sachet gelatine crystals*
*1/2 bottle dry white wine*
*2 tsp lemon juice*

## CHIVE BUTTER

*2 tbsp finely chopped chives*
*4 oz (110g) softened butter*
*A little salt and milled white pepper*
*2 tsp lemon juice*

Boil the quails' eggs for 3 minutes, then cool under running water. Shell carefully, cut in half with a clean stainless steel knife (carbon steel taints). Shell all the fish and cut the flesh into bite-sized pieces.

Make up the aspic jelly as instructed. Cool, but don't allow to set. Bring the white wine to the boil, remove from the heat and sprinkle in half the gelatine crystals. Add 2 teaspoons of lemon juice. Cool. Add *half* the aspic jelly to *all* the wine jelly. (Discard the other half.)

Select individual straight or stemmed glasses that will hold 5 fluid ounces (150 ml). Pack with the fish and halved quails' eggs, sprinkling with chopped chives and a little milled pepper as you layer everything. Try to arrange the halved eggs so you can see their shape and colour through the sides of the glasses.

Put to chill. Then ladle the cool jelly over until the fish is completely covered. I like the jelly to be softish: if, however, you want to show off and turn them out onto plates, then use the whole sachet of gelatine crystals.

Serve with lemon wedges and brown bread and chive butter, which you make by mashing all the ingredients together well on a board or plate. It will keep well in the refrigerator, or may be frozen. These quantities should make enough to butter 8 slices of bread.

# POULTRY AND GAME

◇

*Roast chicken is no longer a Sunday treat; even duckling and game are more reasonably priced than ever before, and turkey joints are readily and reasonably available.* ✦ *To suit the trend towards elegant eating and simpler serving, I have eliminated the laborious job of carving from my recipes. Instead I suggest boning out chickens, using the breasts only of duck, and carving thin escalopes from a young turkey breast. Once the technique of boning is mastered, it is (almost) child's play.* ✦ *The faint-hearted, though, must fall back on the good nature of their poulterer or butcher!*

# ROAST STUFFED DOUBLE CHICKEN BREAST WITH GLAZED CHESTNUTS, BACON STICKS AND CREAMY BREAD SAUCE

*Serves 5–6*

✧

*1 × 4 lb (1.8 kg) chicken*

## FOR THE STUFFING

*The 2 fillets from the chicken, cut up (see method)*
*4 oz (110 g) streaky plain bacon, rindless, roughly chopped*
*1 egg, beaten*
*¼ tsp ground mace*
*1 dsp lemon juice (see method)*
*1 level tsp salt*
*½ tsp milled pepper*
*Butter or oil for frying (see method)*
*10 oz (275 g) chestnuts in brine or in syrup, rinsed under cold water*
*1 tbsp thick cream*

## TO ROAST THE CHICKEN

*2 oz (50 g) soft butter*
*Salt and milled pepper*
*1 tsp ground mace*
*½ clove garlic, crushed (optional)*

Preheat the oven to gas mark 7, 425°F (220°C).

Remove the legs from the chicken and reserve for grilling. Bone out the breasts, keeping the two sides together. Tackle this in the normal manner, taking care after you have removed the flesh on one side of the rib carcass that you do not tear the flesh on the edge of the breast bone as you 'go over the top' to remove the breast meat on the other side. You can leave the wing bones and wish-bone, if the thought of removing these is too daunting! There will – or should be – enough spare skin for you to wrap round when you come to put in the stuffing. Remove the two 'fillets' for use in the stuffing. These are the two almost separate sections of breast meat on each side.

Prepare the stuffing. In a food processor, make a fine purée of the chicken, bacon, egg and seasonings. Scrape into a basin, mix in the cream and half the chestnuts roughly crushed. (If using chestnuts in syrup, add a little lemon juice to counteract the richness.) Retain the rest for glazing (see below).

Open the boned chicken breasts out flat. Season the flesh with salt, milled pepper and a drop or two of lemon juice. Wet your hands and arrange a thick mound of the stuffing down the centre of the breast. Wrap over the chicken, press to a nice chicken shape and sew a seam with linen thread. Any remaining stuffing should be formed into 4 cakes and roasted round the chicken for 20 minutes, or fried in a little butter or oil for 2–3 minutes on each side.

Make a paste with the butter, the teaspoon of mace, seasoning and garlic (if used) and rub all over the chicken skin. Put a small (6 × 6 inch: 15 × 15 cm) piece of foil in the bottom of a roasting tin just large enough to contain the bird. Stand the chicken on this (this will help you remove the chicken from the tin without it sticking). Roast in the preheated oven for 40–45 minutes. Serve in ¼ inch (0.5 cm) slices cut on the diagonal with the bacon sticks and the glazed chestnuts. Arrange any spare forcemeat (stuffing) cakes around, and serve with creamy bread sauce (see p. 124).

## TO MAKE THE BACON STICKS

You will need 8 rindless rashers of streaky bacon. Butter 8 metal skewers and put to set (this is so that the bacon 'grips'). 'Stretch' the rashers with the flat of a knife, and wrap one round each skewer in a spiral. Grill, turning to ensure even browning. Ease the cooked bacon off the skewers with the tines of a fork.

## GLAZE FOR THE CHESTNUTS

*8 chestnuts in syrup, drained, or cooked fresh chestnuts, or chestnuts in brine*

*4 fl oz (100 ml) tinned chicken consommé*

*4 fl oz (100 ml) tomato juice*

*½ oz (10 g) butter*

*2 fl oz (50 ml) dry sherry*

*Salt and pepper*

Put all the ingredients into a non-stick pan and bubble until sticky and viscous. Put in the chestnuts and shake the pan over a low heat to coat them and heat them through.

# CHICKEN-STUFFED BELGIAN ENDIVE WITH BASIL AND PISTACHIO NUTS

*Serves 2*

2 plump heads endive

1 dsp caster sugar

Juice of ½ lemon

6 oz (175 g) raw chicken breast

1 egg, beaten

2 oz (50 g) pistachio nuts, crushed (or use roughly chopped almonds)

4 fl oz (100 ml) double cream, chilled

1 level tsp salt

Milled white pepper

1 small bunch of basil, or chopped chives

## SAUCE

½ pint (275 ml) chicken stock

¼ tsp finely grated lemon rind

2 tsp lemon juice

¼ pint (150 ml) double cream

Salt and milled white pepper

4 large basil leaves, finely shredded

Preheat the oven to gas mark 6, 400°F (200°C).

Trim the endives and cut in half lengthways, but only halfway through. Blanch for 3–4 minutes in a pan of lightly salted boiling water to which you have added the caster sugar and the juice of half a lemon. Cool under running water. Drain well. Open out flat and leave to cool completely.

In a blender make a fine purée of the chicken breast and the egg. Add the chopped herbs as you go along, and season well. Scrape into a bowl, mix in the nuts. Chill for an hour. Now beat in the double cream slowly: you should have a stiffish purée. Pile on to one of the opened-out endives, cut side up. Cover with the second, cut side down. Place in a deep baking dish just large enough to contain it.

Make the sauce by boiling the cream and stock together with the lemon rind and juice; reduce to ½ pint (275 ml). Add the basil and season well. Pour over the endives. Bake in the preheated oven for 30–35 minutes. When ready, remove the stuffed endive from the dish with a flat pierced lifter, spear with a cook's fork and cut crossways in 6 slices. Spoon a little of the rich sauce over.

# SPICED BREAST OF CHICKEN WITH WHISKY AND PINEAPPLE

*Serves 4*

4 chicken breasts, skinned and boned

1 oz (25 g) butter

1 level tsp mild Madras curry powder

½ tsp ground mace

½ tsp ground ginger

1 tsp salt

Milled pepper

½ fresh pineapple, peeled, cored and cut into inch (2.5 cm) 'fans'

¼ pint (150 ml) unsweetened pineapple juice

1 sherry glass of whisky

In a cup mix all the spices together with the salt. Melt the butter in a heavy-based frying pan, until foaming, swirling it around to ensure it doesn't burn at the edges. Fry over a good heat to seal the chicken breasts on each side. Lower the heat and continue frying for 8 minutes or more, depending on their thickness; turn them at 1-minute intervals or thereabouts. Remove the pan from the heat. Transfer the chicken pieces to a warm serving dish. Return the pan to the heat. Add the pineapple pieces and fry them until golden. Pour over the whisky and ignite. When the flames have subsided, pour in the juice and simmer until sticky.

Cut each succulent breast into 4 or 5 diagonal slices. Fan these pieces out onto warm dinner plates, spoon over some of the pineapple sauce, and serve with buttered noodles, rice, or wild rice.

# DOUBLE CHICKEN BREASTS STUFFED WITH SPINACH, COTTAGE CHEESE AND NIB ALMONDS

*Serves 12*

*6 double chicken breasts, boned but intact*

*1 onion, sliced*

*2 oz (50 g) mushrooms, sliced*

*½ bottle dry white wine*

*¾ pint (400 ml) double cream*

*2 tsp lemon juice*

*2 tbsp oil and 1 oz (25 g) butter for frying*

## STUFFING

*2 × 4 oz (100 g) onions, finely chopped*

*2 oz (50 g) butter*

*2 lb (900 g) spinach, de-veined and washed, or 2 × 10 oz (275 ml) pkts frozen leaf spinach, thawed, drained and roughly chopped*

*2 lb (900 g) cottage or ricotta cheese*

*1 teacup finely chopped parsley*

*¼ tsp ground nutmeg*

*8 oz (225 g) nib almonds, browned*

*2 eggs, beaten*

Make the stuffing first. Measure out 6 oz (175 g) of the cottage or ricotta cheese and 2 oz (50 g) of the browned nib almonds and put on one side. Cook the spinach (if using fresh) in an abundance of boiling salted water for 1 minute only. Drain, cool under running cold water, drain again and leave to drain completely in a colander with a weighted plate on top. Chop roughly.

Fry the onion in a covered pan over a low heat in the 2 ounces (50 g) of butter until transparent. Mix in the chopped spinach, the remaining cottage or ricotta cheese and nib almonds, and the chopped parsley. Season well with the nutmeg, salt and milled pepper. Bind with the beaten egg.

Open out the chicken breasts flat, skin side down, on a clean work surface. Season with salt and pepper. Divide the stuffing equally between the breasts. Fold over and tuck in any spare skin. Tie with linen thread in 3 or 4 places to hold together. It doesn't matter if some of the stuffing oozes out.

Preheat the oven to gas mark 7, 425°F (220°C). Heat the butter and oil in a large frying pan. Lightly brown the stuffed chicken breasts on both sides. Brown the onion and mushrooms in the residue fats. Transfer the vegetables to a large shallow flameproof oven dish and arrange the chicken breasts on top in one layer. Pour in the wine. Cook in the oven for 40 minutes. 15 minutes before the end of this time, spread a little of the reserved cheese on top of each breast, and sprinkle with a few of the reserved almonds.

Remove the breasts, slice each one into 5–8 serving pieces and arrange in a warm serving dish (or you can slice the breast at the table. Strain the winy pan juices into a 2 pint (1.1 litre) pan. Reduce to ½ pint (275 ml) by boiling rapidly. Add the cream and boil for a further 10 minutes. Check the seasoning and add 2 teaspoons of lemon juice. Pour into a sauceboat and dribble a little of the rich sauce over the sliced chicken.

# *F*RICASSEE OF CHICKEN WITH VEGETABLES

*Serves 4*

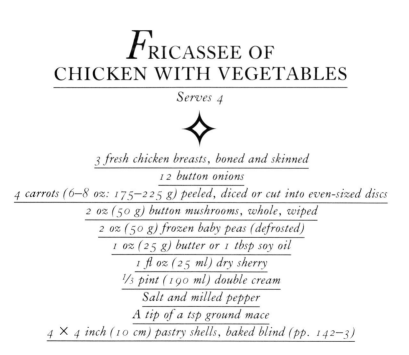

3 fresh chicken breasts, boned and skinned

12 button onions

4 carrots (6–8 oz: 175–225 g) peeled, diced or cut into even-sized discs

2 oz (50 g) button mushrooms, whole, wiped

2 oz (50 g) frozen baby peas (defrosted)

1 oz (25 g) butter or 1 tbsp soy oil

1 fl oz (25 ml) dry sherry

⅓ pint (190 ml) double cream

Salt and milled pepper

A tip of a tsp ground mace

4 × 4 inch (10 cm) pastry shells, baked blind (pp. 142–3)

## *T*O GARNISH

2 tomatoes, skinned, deseeded and cut into dice

1 tbsp flat-leafed parsley, picked and roughly chopped

Cut each chicken breast into 5 or 6 diagonal strips. Melt the butter in a shallow pan until foaming and giving off an almondy smell. Quickly fry the chicken in two batches until *lightly* brown on all sides. Remove to a plate with a slotted spoon.

Fry the onions until they also have taken on a little colour. Return the chicken to the pan, pour in the sherry. Season lightly with salt, 6–8 twists of the pepper mill, and the mace. Add the mushrooms and cream. Bubble, uncovered, for 5–6 minutes, stirring from time to time. When cooked, mix in the carrots and peas (which should be uncooked) and bubble for a further minute to heat through.

Spoon into the pastry shells and scatter the cold tomato dice and parsley over.

*Note*    If the sauce looks oily, add a spoonful of boiling water and mix in.

# *M*INCED CHICKEN WITH RICE
### *Serves 2*

*T*HE Americans have got it about right when they refer to 'minced' meat as 'ground' beef; for that is what it is – the meat has been through a mill. Our word 'mince' is misused, for it stems from the old French *mincier* – to cut small – which in turn comes from the Latin *minutiare*, from which we get minutiae: and this is exactly what I have done in this recipe – cut the chicken meat small. It could not be simpler to prepare, nor, in my opinion, better to eat.

*2 chicken breasts, skinned and boned*
*4 plump spring onions, trimmed but with 2 inches (5 cm) of green left on*
*2 oz (50 g) butter*
*4 fl oz (100 ml) single cream*
*¼ tsp ground coriander*
*Salt and milled pepper*
*Water (see method)*

With a slim, sharp knife cut the chicken breasts into matchstick strips: a labour for which you will be well rewarded! Cut the onions into inch

(2.5 cm) pieces on the diagonal, to make them look more attractive. Melt the butter, swirling it round the pan as it foams. As soon as it goes quiet, add the chicken striplets. Over a high heat, work a straight-edged spatula around to separate and seal the pieces. Season them with the ground coriander, salt and pepper as you go along. Fry for 2 minutes or so — *no more*. Pour in the cream and stir well in, adding the onions. Lower the heat and allow to bubble until everything is well coated. Should the sauce appear to go oily, add a spoonful of water and stir in. This will restore the emulsion. This will only take another minute or two. Serve immediately with plain boiled rice, which you should have ready, or on top of dry breakfast toast without the crusts.

# ROAST CHICKEN WITH WESTPHALIA HAM, CRACKED WHEAT AND CELERY STUFFING

*Serves 5–6*

*4–5 lb (1.8–2.3 kg) chicken or capon, boned*

*4–5 bacon rashers*

*2 oz (50 g) butter*

*Salt and milled pepper*

*1 onion, roughly chopped*

*1 carrot, peeled and roughly chopped*

## FOR THE STUFFING

*2 oz (50 g) cracked or bulghur wheat*

*1 pint (570 ml) chicken stock*

*1½ oz (40 g) butter*

*6 oz (175 g) celery, finely diced*

*2 oz (50 g) spring onions, trimmed and finely chopped*

*6 oz (175 g) Westphalia ham, diced (or another cured ham or a dry salami)*

*1 clove garlic, crushed*

*1 chicken breast, skinned and minced twice*

*1 large egg, beaten*

*Salt and milled pepper*

*A little lemon juice*

## SAUCE

*1 heaped tsp tomato purée*

*4 fl oz (100 ml) dry white wine*

*¼ pint (150 ml) chicken stock*

*¼ pint (150 ml) double cream*

*Residue stock from drained cracked wheat*

Preheat the oven to gas mark 7, 425°F (220°C). Prepare the stuffing first. Pour the stock over the wheat and leave to swell for an hour. Drain, squeeze dry, retaining any unabsorbed liquor for the sauce. Melt the butter in a frying pan without it colouring, so swirl it around. Soften the celery and spring onions for 3–4 minutes over a medium heat, stirring to prevent colouring. Add the ham and the garlic. Stir in and cook for a minute or so. Remove the pan from the heat and allow to cool. Mix in the drained cracked wheat and the minced chicken breast, bind with the beaten egg and season.

Open out the chicken and season the inside lightly with salt, milled pepper and a few drops of lemon juice. Pile the stuffing down the centre, fold the leg meat over. Form into a neat shape resembling a chicken. Tie at 1 inch (2.5 cm) intervals, or slide the stuffed chicken into a piece of tubular butcher's net after seasoning the skin, rubbing all over with butter, and covering with the bacon slices.

Make a cushion of the onion and carrot in a roasting tin just large enough to contain the chicken. Place the chicken on top and roast for 40 minutes, then lower the heat to gas mark 5, 375°F (190°C) for a further 40 minutes, or longer if you like things very well done. Remove the chicken to a warm serving dish. Cut and pull away the strings. Stand the roasting pan on a burner, turn up the heat and fry the vegetables until they are a good brown, adding the tomato purée to make the sauce as you do so.

Drain away any excess fats. Pour in the white wine and work any residues well in. Pour in the stock and allow to bubble for 2–3 minutes. Strain into a small pan, pressing the residues well to extract all the goodness. Reduce this liquid by boiling rapidly to ¼ pint (150 ml). Add the cream and residue stock from the cracked wheat, allow to boil until you have about ⅓ pint (190 ml) of sauce. Serve this separately with the roast chicken.

# ROAST CHICKEN WITH HAM AND CHESTNUT STUFFING

*Serves 5–6*

*1 boned chicken, prepared as in previous recipe*

*8 oz (225 g) lean gammon, minced twice*
*1 large egg, beaten*
*2 fl oz (50 ml) double cream*
*8 oz (225 g) chestnuts, peeled, or chestnuts in brine, drained*
*4 oz (110 g) spring onions, finely chopped, softened in 1 oz (25 g) butter*
*Milled pepper (the ham will probably be salty enough)*
*1/2 tsp mace*
*2 tsp grated orange zest*

## FOR THE GRAVY

*Pan residues*
*1 tsp tomato purée*
*1 level tsp flour*
*2 fl oz (50 ml) Amontillado sherry*
*1/3 pint (190 ml) chicken stock*

Put the minced raw gammon into a blender and purée it with the beaten egg. Season with the milled pepper, orange zest and mace. Scrape into a bowl. Beat in the cream, a little at a time. The mixture should be stiffish. Mix in the spring onions and the roughly chopped chestnuts. Proceed to stuff and roast the chicken as in the previous recipe.

When ready, remove the chicken to a warm serving dish. To make a good gravy, fry the vegetables left in the roasting pan, adding the tomato purée and 1 level teaspoon of flour as you go along. Pour in 2 fluid ounces (50 ml) of Amontillado sherry and 1/3 pint (190 ml) of chicken stock. Bubble for 2 minutes, then strain into a small pan. Leave to stand for 10 minutes. Skim off any excess fats. Reheat the gravy and serve.

# BREASTS OF CHICKEN WITH PECANS AND APPLES AND STILTON SAUCE

*Serves 4*

*4 chicken breasts, skinned and boned*

*2 oz (50 g) butter plus 1 tsp*

*1 tbsp oil*

*1 level tsp ground mace*

*Salt and milled pepper*

*1 oz (25 g) onion, very finely chopped*

*4 fl oz (100 ml) dry white wine or cider*

*⅓ pint (190 ml) single cream*

*2 oz (50 g) ripe Stilton, crumbled*

*2 Cox's apples, peeled, cored and cut into 16 wedges*

*16 pecan (or walnut) halves*

*Juice of 1 small lemon*

In a heavy frying pan melt and evenly heat the oil and 1 ounce (25 g) of butter until foaming. Fry the chicken pieces over a medium heat for 3–4 minutes on each side, seasoning with mace, salt and pepper as they cook, and turning them at 1-minute intervals. Remove the pieces to a warm serving dish.

Add the onion to the pan and soften without letting it take on too much colour. Pour in the wine and let it bubble until reduced to ⅛ pint (75 ml – 2–3 tablespoonfuls). Add the cream and the Stilton. Lower the heat and allow the sauce to bubble, stirring it until it is the consistency of pouring cream: if it is too thick add a spoonful of stock or water. Season again if necessary, adding a good squeeze of lemon juice.

Heat ½ teaspoon of butter in a small pan, toss the pecans in this, salting them lightly as you warm them through and crisp them. Melt the remaining ounce of butter in another frying pan or other shallow pan. Add the apple pieces in one layer, season them lightly with salt, pepper, a dredge or two of ground mace and a tablespoonful of lemon juice. Lower the heat, cover and cook until tender (whisk any residue juices into the sauce). The apples and pecans can be prepared well in advance and put to warm through in the oven at the last minute. To serve, strain the sauce over the chicken pieces, and arrange the apple and walnuts over.

# GRILLED SPRING CHICKEN WITH GRAPEFRUIT, GINGER, HONEY AND HERBS

*Serves 4*

*2 × 1 ½ lb (700 g) chicken, cut in half*

## FOR THE MARINADE

*4 tbsp grape-seed oil*

*1 tbsp grapefruit or lemon juice*

*1 level tsp salt*

*1 level tsp ground coriander, or ginger, or milled pepper*

*1 clove garlic, crushed*

*1 tbsp flower honey*

## TO GARNISH

*2 grapefruits, knife-segmented*

*1 level tbsp roughly chopped coriander leaves*

*1 level tbsp roughly chopped flat-leafed parsley*

*1 level tbsp snipped chives*

*2 pieces stem ginger, finely sliced*

Mix all the ingredients for the marinade in a large bowl. Have your poulterer halve the chickens for you and chop away most of the backbone. Leave the halved chickens in the marinade for 2 hours or more, or overnight.

Preheat the grill to a high heat. Lightly brush the grill pan with oil. Set the pan about 6 inches (15 cm) from the heat and grill the chicken halves, best sides up first, for 3–4 minutes. Turn them and cook for a similar length of time on their insides. Lower the heat and continue to grill them, turning at 1 minute intervals, until they are brown, succulent and to your liking – depending on their size and on your particular grill, this will take 12–14 minutes overall. The honey will caramelise a little. This is intended. Brush with the marinade during grilling.

Half a minute or so before serving, arrange 3 or 4 grapefruit segments on top of each chicken half. Warm them through a little, and sprinkle with fresh herbs when arranged on the serving plates or dish, and with the sliced ginger pieces. This recipe is also ideal for a summer barbecue.

*Note* The spring chickens (or poussins as we wrongly call them) should weigh a minimum of 1½ pounds (700 g) if they are to serve 2. Anything less than this and you should allow one whole bird, i.e. 2 halves, per serving.

# *C*HICKEN SAUSAGES

### *16–18 sausages*

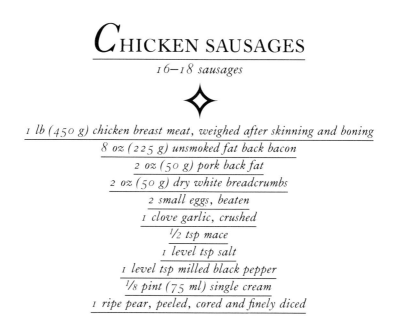

*1 lb (450 g) chicken breast meat, weighed after skinning and boning*

*8 oz (225 g) unsmoked fat back bacon*

*2 oz (50 g) pork back fat*

*2 oz (50 g) dry white breadcrumbs*

*2 small eggs, beaten*

*1 clove garlic, crushed*

*½ tsp mace*

*1 level tsp salt*

*1 level tsp milled black pepper*

*⅛ pint (75 ml) single cream*

*1 ripe pear, peeled, cored and finely diced*

## *B*READ SAUCE WITH CREAM

*1 oz (25 g) butter*

*2 oz (50 g) onion, skinned and chopped*

*½ small clove garlic, crushed*

*1½ oz (40 g) white breadcrumbs*

*⅓ pint (190 ml) rich milk*

*¼ pint (150 ml) double cream*

*¼ tsp ground mace*

*Salt*

In a food processor purée the chicken, bacon, pork fat and breadcrumbs as finely as you can, using the eggs as liquid. Scrape into a bowl. Beat in the garlic and seasonings, with the cream; mix in the diced pear. Fill into sausage skins if you have the necessary attachment on your mincer to do this. Deft-handed people can also do this by using a pastry bag fitted with a broad plain nozzle, but a good alternative is to spoon out tablespoonfuls of the mixture, dipping the spoon in water between each spoonful, onto a lightly floured board before rolling them into sausage shapes.

Fry the sausages in a little clarified butter or light oil, turning them frequently until golden-brown and cooked to your liking. Serve with the creamy bread sauce: in the top of a double boiler over a low flame, melt the butter without colouring it. Soften the onion in this, also without allowing it to colour. Return the pan to its water-filled base, add the milk, bread-crumbs and garlic. Simmer, covered, for 30–40 minutes. Blend to a fine purée and season. Finally, stir in the cream, reheat and serve. The sauce should 'flow' like pouring cream. If it is too thick – this depends on the quality of bread used – add a little more hot milk. ('Plastic' sliced bread should not be used for this since it produces a glutinous sauce.)

# *P*OT-ROAST CHICKEN BREASTS NELL GWYNN WITH ORANGE AND MUSHROOM SAUCE

*Serves 4*

*4 chicken breasts, skinned and boned, leaving the wing bone*

*8 rashers green (plain) streaky bacon, rindless*

*2 tbsp olive oil*

## STUFFING

*2 oz (50 g) butter, softened*

*2 tsp finely grated orange zest*

*1 small clove garlic, crushed*

*¼ tsp ground mace*

*Salt and milled pepper*

*2 knife-segmented oranges, yielding 12–16 segments*

## ORANGE AND MUSHROOM SAUCE

*1 tbsp olive oil*

*2 shallots, finely chopped*

*1 tsp tomato purée*

*1 level tsp plain white flour*

*½ pint (275 ml) strong chicken stock (p. 23)*

*¼ pint (150 ml) dry white wine*

*4 oz (110 g) mushrooms, peeled and very finely chopped*

*2 oz (50 g) butter*

*Chiffonnade of 1 orange, blanched in boiling water*

*Salt and milled white pepper*

*4 oz (110 g) extra unsalted butter, softened (optional)*

Make a savoury paste with the butter, mace, orange zest, garlic, salt and pepper. Remove the fillet from the underside of each breast. With a wetted rolling pin, very gently flatten the breasts and the 'fillets' without breaking up the flesh (the water prevents 'dragging'). Spread each all over with a portion of the savoury paste. Put 4 or 5 segments of orange down the centre of each breast. Cover with the 'fillet', and form into a roll. Wrap round the bacon rashers, overlapping slightly, and spiralling down to the tip. Refrigerate to firm them up for an hour or more. (This job can be done the day before, in which case cover with plastic film.)

Heat the oven to gas mark 9, 475°F (240°C). Melt the 2 oz (50 g) of butter in a heavy-bottomed cast-iron pot large enough to contain the 4 breasts in one layer. Brown them quickly on all sides, using a palette knife and cook's fork to help you. Put *unlidded* into the oven and roast for 20 minutes only, lowering the temperature after 10 minutes to gas mark 7, 425°F (220°C).

Remove, drain, serve whole or sliced diagonally into 4 or 5 slices for each plate, with the Orange and Mushroom Sauce: in a pan, heat the oil until *lightly* smoking. Fry the shallots until soft but not brown. Stir in the modicum of flour and the tomato purée, fry for ½ minute or so, stirring to prevent burning. Pour in the stock and wine, and simmer until reduced to ½ pint (275 ml).

In a second pan heat the butter until it is giving off an 'almondy' aroma, and foaming. Stir in the mushrooms and fry for a minute over a low heat. Strain this over the first mixture, season lightly, and simmer for 3–4 minutes. Make the chiffonnade of orange zest by cutting it meticulously into inchlong (2.5 cm) hair-fine threads and blanching for 1 minute. Add to the sauce and keep it hot in a double boiler, or by putting the sauce in a basin over simmering water, and covering the surface of the sauce with a circle of buttered paper to prevent a skin forming. To enrich the sauce even further, bring it to the boil, remove the pan from the heat, and before adding the chiffonnade, very briskly whisk in the softened butter knob by knob. The sauce will 'mount', or increase, in volume. If this is done, the sauce must *not* be returned to the heat but should be served immediately after adding the chiffonnade.

# *R*OAST PHEASANT WITH GINGER AND ORANGE

*Serves 4*

1 brace pheasant

2 tbsp olive or soy oil

2 oz (50 g) butter

3 tsp ground ginger

2 tsp (or less) salt

Milled pepper

1 leek, cleaned and sliced

2 cloves garlic, crushed

1 carrot, peeled and diced

1 onion, skinned and chopped

2 oz (50 g) mushrooms, wiped and sliced

1 level tsp flour

1 fl oz (25 ml) whisky

1/4 pint (150 ml) double cream

## *TO* GARNISH

1 large Jaffa or navel orange, knife-peeled and segmented

2 pieces stem or green ginger, finely sliced

Preheat the oven to gas mark 8, 450°F (230°C). Using a large serrated knife or game shears, cut the birds in half, and then cut away the back bone as best you can. Season well inside and outside with salt and pepper.

In a pan wide enough to hold the four halves (or in two batches), heat the oil and butter until foaming and giving off a light haze. Fry the pheasant on both sides for 2–3 minutes, when it should look a good golden-brown. Fry the back-bone pieces as well. Dredge or sprinkle over the ground ginger and a little more salt as you go along. Remove the pieces from the pan.

In the residue fats, soften and lightly brown the vegetables and garlic. Transfer these and the back bones to a roasting tin, spreading them out as a bed of vegetables on which to lay the four pheasant halves.

Roast the pheasant in the preheated oven for 30–45 minutes, depending on how well done you like game. Transfer to a warm serving dish and keep hot in the oven at gas mark 1, 275°F (140°C). Stand the roasting pan over a high heat, sprinkle over the modicum of flour, and mix and stir the vegetables until they are well coloured. Pour over the whisky, ignite, and let the flames subside. Pour in the cream, together with a teacup of water. Simmer for 5 minutes. Strain through a fine-meshed sieve into a small pan. Boil the sauce until it looks glossy. (If it looks oily, add a spoonful of water.) Add the stem ginger, pour the sauce around the waiting pheasant, and garnish with the orange segments. Serve with wild rice, noodles or new potatoes.

# *B*UTTER-ROAST PARTRIDGE
# WITH MADEIRA CREAM SAUCE

*Serves 2*

*1 brace partridge*

*4 oz (110 g) softened butter*

*½ clove garlic*

*Smidgen of ground mace*

*½ tsp salt and milled pepper*

*2 rashers bacon*

*2 small slivers onion*

*¼ tsp flour*

*½ tsp tomato purée*

*4 fl oz (100 ml) dry Madeira*

*¼ stock cube*

*¼ pint (150 ml) single cream*

*2 oz (50 g) tin of Swiss parfait*

*2 butter-fried croûtons, 2 inches (5 cm) in diameter*

Preheat the oven to gas mark 9, 475°F (240°C). Make a paste of the butter, garlic, mace, half-teaspoon salt and a few screws of pepper. Rub this all over and inside each bird. Cover the breasts by curling round a rasher of bacon. Sit the birds on a sliver of onion in a small compact roasting tin and roast near the top of the oven for 15 minutes, then lower the heat to gas mark 7, 425°F (220°C) for a further 15–20 minutes, depending how pink you like your game. Remove the birds and keep warm.

Pour away any excess fats. Sprinkle in ¼ teaspoon flour – no more. Let this brown, with the modest amount of tomato purée, over a low heat. Crumble in quarter of a stock cube, add the Madeira, and bring to the boil. Reduce the heat and simmer for 2 minutes, adding the cream at this point. Strain into a warm sauceboat, or pour on to dinner plates. Stand each partridge on a butter-fried croûton spread with Swiss parfait.

# $F$RICASSEE OF TURKEY WITH SMOKED EEL AND SOURED APPLES

*Serves 4*

*1½ lb (700 g) raw boned breast of turkey cut into 2 inch (5 cm) strips*

*8 oz (225 g) fresh smoked eel fillets, cut likewise*

*4 fl oz (100 ml) Amontillado sherry*

*4 fl oz (100 ml) single cream*

*2 oz (50 g) unsalted butter*

*2 green apples*

*Juice of ½ lemon*

*Salt and milled pepper*

*Egg noodles to accompany*

Peel, core and trim the apples, and cut in 6 wedges. Toss in the lemon juice, and drop them, including the lemon juice, into boiling salted water; simmer for 1½ minutes. Drain, and put to one side.

Heat half the butter and fry the turkey pieces in it, in 2 or 3 batches, until lightly browned, turning them all the time to ensure even colouring. Transfer each batch to a warm dish (add more butter to the pan as needed). Pour the sherry into the pan and let it bubble well for a minute or so. Pour in the cream and let it bubble more until beginning to thicken. Check the season-ing. Carefully mix in the strips of turkey and smoked eel and heat through until well coated with the sauce. Serve garnished with the apples on a bed of buttered noodles.

# *A* WARM
# SALAD OF QUAIL

*Serves 4*

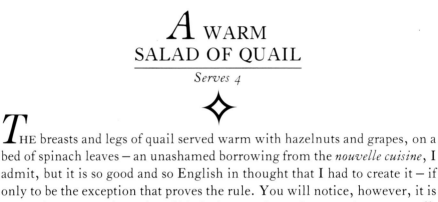

*T*HE breasts and legs of quail served warm with hazelnuts and grapes, on a bed of spinach leaves — an unashamed borrowing from the *nouvelle cuisine*, I admit, but it is so good and so English in thought that I had to create it — if only to be the exception that proves the rule. You will notice, however, it is somewhat more robust than if it had come from the 'mosaic' or *nouvelle* kitchens!

*4 quails*

*2 oz (50 g) butter*

*¼ tsp mace*

*Salt and milled pepper*

*2 fl oz (50 ml) Amontillado sherry*

*16–20 large grapes, skinned, pipped and halved*

*Young, washed spinach leaves, with the veins removed*

*Hazelnuts, toasted, skinned, and roughly crushed*

## FOR THE DRESSING

*2 tbsp walnut or hazelnut oil*

*1 tbsp sherry, vinegar, or red wine vinegar*

*Salt and milled pepper*

*The pan juices*

Preheat the oven to gas mark 9, 475°F (240°C). In a cast-iron ramekin just large enough to hold the quails, heat the butter until foaming hot, and then quickly brown the quails on all sides. Season with salt, brown pepper and mace. Transfer the pan to the oven and roast for 10 minutes only.

Remove the quail. Pour the 2 fluid ounces (50 ml) of sherry into the roasting dish and reduce by boiling on top of the stove to 1 tablespoonful. Scrape the pan juices through a small sieve into the bowl in which you will make the dressing. Add the dressing ingredients and mix well.

Gently pull the legs from each quail and chop off the feet or remove with a pair of kitchen scissors. Take the breasts off by cutting down either side of the breast bone and easing the pink meat away. Cut each breast into 3 slices on the diagonal. Arrange 6 to 8 spinach leaves on each plate. Place the quail meat attractively on top. Garnish with the grapes. Warm the dressing in a small pan: splash over the salad and sprinkle with the crushed hazelnuts. Serve warm.

# *R*OAST DUCKLING WITH APPLE, SAGE AND ONION PURÉE

*Serves 4*

✦

*I*'VE always been a believer that if I think, feel, need or enjoy something, then there's a good chance that a reasonable number of other folk will be of a similar mind. Those who enjoy *nouvelle cuisine* in all its Frenchness will have come across the by now almost ubiquitous *magret* of duckling. For an Englishman, this is surely anathema, for doesn't duckling have to be roasted to a crisp turn? I'm happy to meet this trend halfway in this recipe, which uses either duckling or duck. If you like, you can remove the legs to make a terrine or braise for a family meal on some other day, but as I enjoy the thighs perhaps even more than the breast, in spite of the knife-work involved in eating them, I will personally continue to roast the whole bird.

So, let's move ahead with the times. Here I suggest two 3 pound (1.4 kg) birds for four people and I have brought this recipe into the realms of the sublime by marrying the three essential English accompaniments to duck — sage, onion, apple — into one delicious sauce: no other gravy or accompaniment is required. Serve it with creamed leeks, a purée of peas and, of course, new potatoes. I think you'll agree this new way *is* elegant!

*2 × 2½–3 lb (1.1–1.4 kg) duckling (or 1 larger duck) with or without their legs!*

## BUTTER PASTE

*4 oz (110 g) butter, softened*

*1 clove garlic, crushed*

*1 tsp rubbed sage*

*1 tsp rubbed thyme*

*1 tsp salt*

*1 tsp milled black pepper*

## APPLE, SAGE AND ONION PURÉE

*1 oz (25 g) butter or soy oil*

*1/2 medium onion, chopped*

*Small clove garlic, crushed*

*3/4 lb (350 g) Cox's apples, peeled, cored and chopped*

*1/8 pint (75 ml) reduced stock or 1/8 pint water and 1 chicken stock cube*

*1 tbsp fresh sage, chopped or 2 tsp dried sage*

*Juice of 1/2 lemon*

*Salt, if necessary, and milled pepper*

Preheat the oven to gas mark 7, 425°F (220°C). Make a paste of all the ingredients, then — and this may surprise you — prick the skin of the birds all over, not so much to let the fats out (and a duck by nature is a fatty bird, so if you don't enjoy its succulence I timidly suggest you leave well alone) but to get the seasoning *into* the skin and flesh. Rub the skin well and put a little of the paste inside each bird. Stand them on a wire rack in a roasting tin. Roast in the preheated oven for 20 minutes, then lower the temperature to gas mark 5, 375°F (190°C) for a further 25–30 minutes. Leave to stand for 15 minutes.

Prepare the purée. Heat the butter or oil until lightly smoking: add the onion and fry to a golden — not dark — brown, stirring to ensure the edges don't burn. Add the apples, garlic and sage and stir in well. Fry for a minute or so. Add the stock, or crumble in the stock cube, and add the water and lemon juice. Simmer for 20 minutes. Blend when cool, and rub through a fine sieve. Reheat and serve (the sauce can be made the day before).

With a sharp pointed knife, cut down either side of the breast bone of each duck and right down between the wing bone joint where it joins the carcass. Gently cut away the flesh from the breast-bone and release the skin at the base of the duck where it joins the bottom of the carcass. Using the hilt of a large cook's knife, a cleaver, or game shears, cut off the wing bone to within an inch of where it joins the breast section.

Pour a pool of the purée onto warm dinner plates, stand the boned breast on this, tuck a sprig of watercress underneath, and serve.

*Note*   If you decide to take the legs off before cooking, reduce the roasting times to 15 minutes and 20 minutes respectively.

# *B*UTTER-FRIED TURKEY SCALLOPS

*Serves 4*

*4 large or 8 small turkey scallops cut from approx. 1½ lb (700 g) raw turkey breast*

*6 oz (175 g) skinned hazelnuts, finely crushed*

*1 large egg, beaten and seasoned*

*4 oz (110 g) clarified butter (or oil) for frying*

## *O*RANGE HAZELNUT SAUCE

*3 egg yolks*

*1 tsp flower honey*

*¼ pint (150 ml) freshly squeezed orange juice*

*¼ tsp salt*

*Milled white pepper*

*¼ stock cube*

*Zest of 1 orange*

*2 oz (50 g) hazelnuts, lightly toasted and roughly crushed*

*4 oz (110 g) hot melted butter*

Gently beat each scallop with a wetted rolling pin to break down the fibres, taking care not to mash the meat! Pass each one through the beaten egg, and then through the hazelnuts, pressing them well in and shaking away any loose pieces. Heat the butter until it is giving off an almondy or nutty smell. Fry the scallops – 4 at a time – until they are nicely golden-brown on both sides (about 1½ minutes each side). Drain on crumpled kitchen paper, then lightly dust with a smidgen of salt and a twist or two of pepper.

Prepare the sauce: remove the zest from the orange with a potato peeler and laboriously cut it into fine threads. Boil for 1 minute in a little water, drain, rinse under cold water, cool and put on one side.

Arrange a basin over a pan of boiling water. Whisk together, until a firm ribbon forms, the egg yolks, orange juice, honey and stock cube. Remove the basin from the pan: stand it on a damp cloth to prevent skidding, and slowly dribble in, then whisk in, the hot melted butter. Season to taste; add the orange zest and nuts. Invert the lid over a pan of hot water and stand the basin on this to keep warm — the sauce does not need to be served piping hot.

Arrange the scallops on a warm napkin-lined dish or salver, and serve with the sauce.

# *W*ARM DUCK SALAD

*Serves 6*

*A* SALAD which makes one duck go a long way — and you'll still have the legs left to grill for another light meal.

*1 × 4 lb (1.8 kg) duckling, or 4 duck breast portions*

## *F*OR THE MARINADE

*2 tbsp soy sauce*

*1 tbsp dry sherry*

*1 tbsp olive oil*

*1 tbsp orange juice*

*1 tsp salt*

*1 tsp ground coriander*

*1 tsp ground ginger*

*1 tsp ground mace*

*1 clove garlic, crushed*

## *F*OR EACH SERVING OF SALAD

*2 good curly endive leaves*

*2 radicchio leaves*

*1 slice beefsteak tomato*

*2–3 slices cucumber*

*1 artichoke bottom*

*1 black olive, pitted*

## FOR THE DRESSING

*¹/₄ pint (150 ml) olive oil*
*¹/₈ pint (75 ml) orange juice*
*1 tbsp red wine vinegar*
*1 tsp honey*
*¹/₂ tsp salt*
*1 tsp mild French mustard*
*¹/₂ tsp milled black pepper*
*1 tsp finely grated orange rind*

Have your poulterer remove the duck breasts and cut off the legs; keep them to use on another occasion, and keep the carcass to use for stock for beetroot soup (p. 27). Make 5 or 6 shallow incisions into the fleshy side of the breasts, about ¼ inch (0.5 cm) deep, running right across. Arrange, cut sides upmost, in a shallow dish. Mix all the ingredients for the marinade together well and pour over. Now turn the breasts cut sides down and leave for 12 hours, or overnight.

To make the salad, preheat 2 tablespoons of olive oil in a heavy-bottomed frying pan until smoking. Remove the breasts from the marinade and seal on both sides. Lower the heat a little and fry the breasts for 3 minutes on each side if you like the meat to be pink, a little longer if it is to be well done. Remove the breasts to a plate whilst you assemble the salad ingredients on separate plates or dishes and prepare the dressing by shaking all very thoroughly together in a screw-topped jar. Slice the still warm duck breasts in thin diagonal slivers. Arrange 3 or 4 slivers on top of each assembled salad.

A few butter-fried bread croûtons can be added for extra crunch if liked. These too should be warm, or 'tiède', as the French say; the direct translation of 'tepid' sounds rather unappetising to the English ear!

# *R*OAST BONED DUCK LEGS WITH PLUMS

*Serves 4*

*A* DELICIOUS way of using the legs if you have used the breasts in the previous recipe.

*4 duck legs*

*The livers from the ducks (see method)*

*1 tsp finely grated orange zest*

*1 level tsp mild made mustard*

*2 oz (50 g) butter*

*2 tbsp olive or soy oil*

*Salt and milled pepper*

*8 plums, stoned and quartered*

*Sprinkling of dry mustard and sugar*

## PLUM SAUCE

*The giblets (except the liver) and some of the bones
and wing tips from the ducks, cut up into small pieces*

*1 tsp flour*

*1/2 pint (275 ml) stock (use tinned consommé)*

*1/2 pint (275 ml) dry white wine*

*1/4 pint (150 ml) tomato juice*

*3 ripe plums, stoned*

*2–3 sage leaves*

*Tip of a tsp made mustard*

*Salt and pepper*

It is not as difficult as may first appear to bone the legs. Start at the thick (thigh) end of each leg, and fold or roll back the skin and flesh, scraping the flesh away from the bone with a small, sharp, pointed knife as you go along. Roll the meat back as you would do a stocking when taking it off!

When you get to the joint between the drumstick and thigh, cut carefully between the knuckle socket. You may find it easier to clip this away with kitchen scissors. Continue to roll and scrape to the end of the drumstick bone, pull the meat over the last knuckle joint (or chop this off with the hilt of a cook's knife or a cleaver). It will be inside out. Make a paste of the orange zest, mustard, 1 oz (25 g) butter and seasoning, and rub a little into the thick part of the duck flesh. Turn the boned leg right side out again. Prepare the plums for the stuffing and season with salt, milled pepper and a sprinkling of mustard and sugar. Stuff each leg with some of the fruit and sew up with linen thread.

In a skillet, heat 2 tablespoonfuls of oil and 1 ounce (25 g) of butter until lightly smoking. Over a highish heat, seal and brown the legs on all sides.

*Page 137 Steak, Kidney and Mushroom Pie*
*Page 138 Fricassee of Chicken with Vegetables*

Transfer the skillet to the oven, gas mark 6, 400°F (200°C) and roast for 25–30 minutes, turning two or three times during this process. 5 minutes before the end of the cooking time add the whole liver and any remaining fruit.

Drain. Carve each leg into five or six slices. Serve garnished with the odd slices of liver, a few pieces of the fruit and a little of the plum sauce. To prepare this, put the giblets and bones in a roasting tin. Sprinkle evenly with the flour and brown in the oven (turn the heat up to gas mark 8, 450°F (230°C)). This will take 15–20 minutes. Stir them round halfway through. Transfer this débris to a pan. Swill out the tin with the white wine over a low heat on the top of the stove. Add the remaining ingredients, including the débris, but omitting the salt. Simmer for 20 minutes. Strain into a clean pan, rinsing the bones off with a little water. Reduce to ½ pint (275 ml) by boiling rapidly. Salt sparingly and skim off any scum.

*Note*  Chicken legs can be prepared in this way.

# *P*AN-FRIED DUCK BREASTS

*Serves 2*

2 duck breasts (see method)
2 oz clarified butter, or olive or soy oil
Salt and milled pepper
1 tbsp freshly chopped sage

Have your poulterer or butcher remove the breasts, including the wing bone, from a 3 lb (1.4 kg) duck. This will give you 2 large chunks of boneless breast meat, with the skin on.

Melt the butter in a pan until it is almost nutty brown. Put in the breasts, skin down, seal and brown them on both sides over a good heat. Lower the heat and continue cooking – seasoning lightly with salt and pepper as you turn them – for 5–6 minutes on each side. Sprinkle with the fresh sage.

On a board, cut each breast into 5 or 6 slices on the diagonal, and with the knife held at an inward slant. Fan the slices out and arrange on warm dinner plates. Serve with a pool of Apple, Sage and Onion Purée (p. 132).

# RED PEPPER OMELETTES STUFFED WITH TURKEY IN HORSERADISH CREAM SAUCE

*Serves 4*

✦

*P*EPPERS are here to stay, so here is an English way of using them, in a cold savoury omelette.

*3 large eggs*
*½ red pepper, deseeded and cut into minute dice, or coarsely minced*
*1 tbsp thick cream*
*Salt and milled pepper*
*Small knob of butter for frying*

## FOR THE FILLING

*8 fl oz (225 ml) mayonnaise, home-made, or a good commercial brand*
*2 heaped tsp bottled creamed horseradish*
*1 bunch spring onions, trimmed, washed and finely chopped*
*1 lb (450 g) cold turkey meat (breast and/or leg) cut into striplets*
*1 red pepper, deseeded and finely shredded with a knife*
*Salt and milled pepper*

Prepare the filling first. Mix the mayonnaise and creamed horseradish together in a large bowl. Season well. Mix in the remaining ingredients.

To make the omelettes, whisk the eggs, and season well. Stir in the cream and pepper. Heat the butter in a small omelette pan. Make 4 thin omelettes without letting them brown. Cool. Spread each one with the filling, and either fold or roll them up. Serve with a salad.

# MEAT

◆

*At last our butchers are seeing the light and catching on to the truth that we can no longer afford an English roast as a bi-weekly event.*✦ *God forbid that the roast beef of Olde Englande should disappear, but it just has to be kept for a more special occasion. What we want are well-butchered cuts of meat to make the new dishes that I and others have been encouraging you to try. It makes sense to bone out a loin of lamb, cut away excess fat and tie it, ready to cut into delicate 'rounds', every morsel of which can be eaten.*✦ *It makes sense, too, that mince should be fat-free, and that steak should be cut from beef which has been well hung and trimmed of fat, particularly to lift unexciting meat pies and puddings to new culinary heights.*

# $S$TEAK, KIDNEY AND MUSHROOM PIES

*Serves 6–8*

$T$RADITIONALLY this English recipe is palish in colour, therefore the tendency to over-Frenchify it, as has been done in recent years by some cooks, is to be resisted. Long braising in red wine, even the inclusion of tomato purée, has become a habit in our efforts to improve things, but the natural flavour of the three ingredients ought not to be masked. I don't think they are in my revised recipe.

### FOR THE PASTRY SHELLS

*12 oz (350 g) puff or rough puff pastry (commercial brands are excellent)*

### STEAK, KIDNEY AND MUSHROOM MIXTURE

*2 lb (900 g), to yield 1½ lb (700 g), rump or best braising steak, trimmed of all fat and cut into ½ inch (1 cm) cubes*

*2 lambs' kidneys, skinned, trimmed and diced*

*2–3 extra lambs' kidneys for garnish (optional)*

*Oil for frying*

*4 oz (110 g) onion, very finely chopped*

*6 oz (175 g) small white-cap mushrooms, quartered*

*1 oz (25 g) plain flour*

*¾ pint (400 ml) beef stock (or tinned consommé)*

*1 tsp salt*

*Milled white pepper*

Preheat the oven to gas mark 7, 425°F (220°C). Select two individual tins which will fit inside each other. This means they should taper somewhat and be approximately 4 inches (10 cm) in diameter. Brush one inside and the other outside with melted butter. Roll out the pastry in a large oblong, 16 × 12 inches (40.5 × 30.5 cm). Cut into 6 or 8 pieces. Line the tin(s) with one of the pieces and trim off the edges. Prick all over with the tines of a fork. Fit the second tin inside, press well home. (You can use the old foil and bean technique for blind baking, but I think my way is easier and more successful.) Bake in the preheated oven for 15–20 minutes. Cool a little. Remove the top tin and return the shell to the oven if it is not completely crisp and golden-brown. Cool on a wire tray. Store the shells in an airtight container.

Prepare the filling. Heat the oil until smoking. Brown the cubes of beef and kidney in small batches, removing each one when ready to a plate; sprinkle with the flour, stirring well in, and season.

Brown the onion in the residue fats. Return the meats to the pan, pour over the stock. Simmer, stirring from time to time, for 30 minutes or until tender. Add the mushrooms 10 minutes before the end of the cooking time. If you wish to top each serving with kidney, cut the kidneys in half, and fry quickly for a minute or two on each side in a good knob of butter. Season well. Drain, and keep warm.

Reheat the shells at gas mark 1, 275°F (140°C) for a few minutes, fill with the mixture, and serve immediately.

# YORKSHIRE MINCE PLAIT
## WITH PICKLED WALNUTS

*Serves 5–6*

2 lb (900 g) best braising or rump steak, well minced

1 tbsp white flour

4 sticks celery, washed and diced

1 medium onion, skinned and finely chopped

2 tbsp good oil or butter

5–6 pickled walnuts, diced

1 tsp each: ground thyme, mild curry powder, sweet paprika, salt, ground pepper

Scant ½ pint (275 ml) stock or water

3 tbsp dry sherry

1 lb (450 g) puff pastry

1 egg, beaten with a little top of the milk

Heat the oil or butter in a heavy-bottomed pan which will go into the oven. Soften the onion and celery and fry until golden-brown. Gradually incorporate the minced meat, and sprinkle over the flour, working well in with a wooden spatula. Add all the seasonings. Remove the mixture to a basin or tray.

Pour the sherry into the pan and work into the pan sediments until they are all released. Add the stock. Return the mince mixture to the pan, mix well and cover. Cook in the oven at gas mark 6, 400°F (200°C) for 30 minutes. Add the pickled walnuts to the mixture and let it cool. Chill until ready for use.

When ready to make the plait, preheat the oven to gas mark 8, 450°F (230°C). Have the puff pastry defrosted to room temperature. On a lightly-floured board roll the pastry into a rectangle approximately 20 × 16 inches (50 × 40.5 cm). In your mind's eye divide the pastry into 3 equal panels. Cut diagonal slits into the 2 outside panels, to make chevron shapes on either side. Brush all over with beaten egg. Pile the cold, stiffish mince mixture down the uncut centre panel. Fold over the pastry strips alternately, overlapping and tucking each strip under the mince to make a plait. Pinch the ends and top together as best you can. Any pastry trimmings can be rolled out into a long piece, cut into three strips and plaited for decoration. This is laid on top of the filled plait and brushed with further beaten egg.

Slide the plait on to a wetted baking sheet: brush all over with beaten egg, and bake in the preheated oven for 20 minutes. Lower the temperature to gas mark 5, 375°F (190°C) for a further 30–35 minutes, when the pastry should be crisp and golden-brown. Serve hot, warm or cold with extra pickled walnuts and apple chutney.

# $M$INI
## SHEPHERD'S PIES

*Serves 4–5*

*1 lb (450 g) rump steak or leg fillet of lamb minced twice*

*1 tsp plain white flour*

*1 small onion, skinned and finely chopped*

*1 tbsp olive or soy oil*

*1/2 pint (275 ml) red wine*

*1/2 pint (275 ml) beef stock*

*1/4 pint (150 ml) tomato juice*

*Salt and milled white pepper*

*12–16 small potatoes, baked in their jackets (see method)*

## FOR THE TOPPING

*2 parts mashed potato*
*1 part choux pastry (see p. 217)*
*1 tbsp freshly grated Parmesan cheese*

Preheat the oven to gas mark 6, 400°F (200°C). In a heavy fireproof casserole, heat the tablespoon of oil and fry the onion until golden-brown, stirring to prevent burning. Add the mince in small batches, and continue to fry over a *high* heat until all is well sealed. Sprinkle over the modicum of flour, stir it in and fry for a minute or so. Season to taste. Add all the liquids, cover with a lid, and over a *low* heat cook for 30 minutes, stirring from time to time; by now you should have a rich, well-amalgamated mixture. Leave to cool.

Scoop out all the inside from the baked potatoes, leaving just the thin crisp skins. Reserve enough potato to use in the topping, and keep the rest for another day. You should now have 12–16 potato shells: fill each one to the top with the minced beef mixture.

Prepare the topping. Press the reserved potato through a potato ricer and beat well with a little butter and ¼ pint (150 ml) hot milk. The mixture should be fairly firm. Mix with the choux pastry and pipe, spoon or 'fork' the mixture on top of each shell. Sprinkle with a little Parmesan cheese. Bake in the preheated oven until the topping is well puffed up and golden-brown (about 20 minutes). These quantities should give you about 10–12 pies, depending on size – allow 2–3 per serving.

# *P*AN-FRIED FILLET STEAK WITH MUSTARD AND CAPER SAUCE

*Serves 4*

*T*HIS type of 'professional' cookery is by no means beyond the capacity of the average cook. It does, however, have to be prepared as near to serving time as possible. So assemble together all the ingredients for the dish beforehand and cook just before settling your guests at the table for their first course. For 4 people, you will have to fry the fillets in 2 batches, or in 2 pans, unless you have a 12 inch (30.5 cm) frying pan, in which case have a go at doing it in one. Keep the heat high and work quickly; the results will certainly earn you applause!

*8 × ¼ inch (0.5 cm) thick slivers of fillet steak*

*Salt and milled pepper*

*1 oz (25 g) butter*

*2 tbsp olive or soy oil*

*3 fl oz (75 ml) Amontillado sherry*

*1 heaped tsp mild French mustard*

*⅓ pint (190 ml) single cream*

*¼ stock cube, crumbled*

*2 tbsp sweet capers (in brine rather than in vinegar, if possible)*

Ask your butcher to cut the slices from the centre to the thicker end of the fillet: the meat should be trimmed of all fat.

In a heavy-bottomed frying pan heat the oil and butter until it is smoking lightly and has a tan-coloured 'foam'. Swirl the pan round, or stir around with a wooden spatula to ensure an even blending of the two fats. Use a small palette knife and cook's fork to lay the steaks in the pan over a high heat. Leave them to brown for 1–2 minutes. As soon as blood globules start to appear on the upper surface of the steak, season with salt and milled pepper — about 1 teaspoon of salt and the same of black pepper. Turn the steaks over, using the palette knife and fork again (in an ordinary pan, should the albumen from the meat cause sticking, the palette knife will readily slide underneath to release the steaks without tearing the flesh). Fry for only 10 seconds (more if you like steak well done). Remove the pan from the heat. Transfer the steaks to a warm serving dish.

Allow the fats to settle for a few seconds, then pour off any surplus fat, making sure you retain the juices and 'crust'. Return the pan to a high heat; after a few seconds crumble in the piece of stock cube. Pour in the sherry, which will bubble furiously and may ignite. Worry not! Pour in the cream, lower the heat, and work everything together into a delicious mixture, adding the mustard and 2 tablespoons or so of cold water. Scrape and pour the sauce through a sieve into a small pan: let it bubble again until it has cohered and is the consistency of light pouring cream. Stir in the capers. Keep hot by standing this pan in a larger one filled a third of the way up with simmering water.

When you are ready to serve the steaks, spoon the sauce over each. It is rich, so there should be a good coating for each piece. If the sauce looks oily, whisk in a drop or two of water to restore the balance of the emulsion, which is what you have (though perhaps unwittingly) cleverly made.

# STEAK, KIDNEY AND MUSHROOM PUDDING

### Serves 6

$A$s the buttery, yet light, crust is on the top only, weight-watchers need not worry. The simple good flavours of the ingredients should speak for themselves.

*2 lb (900 g) best steak, trimmed of all fat and sinew (I use rump)*

*12 button onions, skinned*

*8 oz (225 g) veal or lamb kidney (not ox)*

*8 oz (225 g) tiny button mushrooms*

*1 clove garlic, cut in half*

*2 sprigs fresh thyme*

*2 tsp white flour*

*1 tsp salt*

*Cold water to cover*

*Very little pepper*

*2 oz (50 g) butter or soy oil for frying*

## FOR THE CRUST

*5 oz (150 g) S.R. flour*

*1 level tsp baking powder*

*3 oz (75 g) cold, hard butter, grated on the coarse side of a grater*

*1 tbsp finely chopped parsley*

*1 tbsp finely grated lemon rind*

*1 level tsp salt*

*A little white pepper, milled*

*1 egg beaten with 2 tbsp cold water*

Heat the oil or butter until it is lightly smoking, and brown the onions. Remove them to a casserole. Toss the meat in the flour and lightly brown it in the pan in small batches, removing each one as finished to the casserole. Season sparingly with salt and a very little pepper. Mix in the mushrooms and the garlic. Cut the kidney into ¼ inch (0.5 cm) slices, and seal them in a little oil or butter; then add these to the rest. Add the thyme.

Pour over enough water just to cover — a pint (570 ml) at most. Cover and simmer over a low heat for an hour, or cook in the oven. Cool. Pour into a 2–3 pint (1.1–1.75 litre) pudding basin.

To make the crust, sift the baking powder and seasonings into the flour, and gently rub in the butter. Mix in the parsley. Using a fork, mix to a softish dough with the egg and water. Turn on to a floured surface and press or roll into a circle which will just fit *inside* the top of the basin. Cover with greaseproof paper, and then with foil — make a deep pleat across and across again so that you have a pocket into which the crust can rise. Tie down well. Place in a large saucepan filled a third of the way up with boiling water, cover and steam at a steady roll for 1½–2 hours.

When ready to serve, cut a wedge of the light crust top, and serve with a spoonful of the filling. This goes very well with steamed, finely shredded savoy cabbage, tossed whilst hot in soured cream and caraway or fennel seeds.

## ALTERNATIVE CHOUX PASTRY TOPPING FOR INDIVIDUAL PUDDINGS

*3 oz (75 g) butter*

*½ pint (275 ml) water*

*5 oz (150 g) plain white flour, sieved with*
*½ tsp salt and milled white pepper*

*4 eggs, beaten*

*1 tbsp snipped chives (or young spring onions)*

*1 tbsp finely chopped, flat-leafed parsley*

Bring the butter and water to the boil in a pan. Remove from the heat and add the flour at one fell swoop. Beat vigorously until the mixture leaves the sides of the pan in one 'clean' ball. Using a wooden spatula, beat in the eggs a little at a time until the mixture is smooth, silky-textured and glossy. Mix in the herbs.

Fill individual pudding basins with the steak and kidney filling, and spoon the choux pastry on top. Cover with greaseproof paper and pleated foil as before and tie down well. Stand the puddings in a water bath, cover this too with a large shell of foil. Cook in the oven at gas mark 6, 400°F (200°C) for 45 minutes. Serve immediately for guests to turn out for themselves.

# BOILED FILLET OF BEEF AND CAPER SAUCE

*Serves 6*

$\diamondsuit$

WHY this one-time traditional dish has not been raised to the heights instead of being allowed to slide into oblivion can only be because of our deep-grained British sense of economy.

*2 pints (1.1 litres) rich beef stock (p. 20 — or use tinned consommé)*

*1½–2 lb (700–900 g) piece of fillet steak*

*1 clove garlic, cut into the thinnest slivers*

*Small bunch of chives, whole*

*1 tbsp each chopped chives and flat-leafed parsley*

*6 young leeks, trimmed and cut in half*

*3 tomatoes, halved*

*6 cauliflower florets*

*12 young carrots, or older ones cut into sticks*

*1 celery heart cut into 6*

*12 button onions*

## RICH CAPER SAUCE

*4 large egg yolks*

*½ pint (275 ml) of the hot cooking liquor, strained*

*2 oz (50 g) good butter cut into small cubes and at room temperature*

*2 tsp (one good squeeze) lemon juice*

*2 tbsp sweet capers, drained*

*1 tbsp snipped chives*

*Salt and milled pepper if needed*

Choose a pan just large enough to hold the piece of fillet steak, which should be rolled and tied securely at 1 inch (2.5 cm) intervals. Use a sharp pointed knife to stab the steak, at least 1½ inches (3.5 cm) deep. Leave the knife in place, and gently press it back to slide 1 sliver of garlic and 2 or 3 chives into the incision. Do this 6 or so times down the length of the fillet.

Bring the stock to boiling point, lower in the fillet, reduce the heat, and simmer for 10 minutes for rare, 20 minutes for more well done. (It takes remarkably little time to cook!) Remove the steak from the stock, cut away the strings and put into a deep, lidded serving dish, to keep warm in a low oven, gas mark 1, 275°F (140°C). Bring the stock back to boiling point and put the vegetables in to cook for 3–4 minutes, leaving them still crisp. Remove with a draining spoon and put round the meat with a ladleful or two of the stock. Sprinkle over the herbs just before serving.

For the sauce, whisk the egg yolks with the hot stock in a basin arranged over a pan of gently boiling water until thick and the whisk leaves a distinct trail. Remove the basin from the heat and briskly whisk in the softened butter. Do not reheat. Stir in the capers, chives and lemon juice, and pour into a warm sauceboat. Carve the meat into ¼ inch (0.5 cm) slices, and serve with some of the vegetables and the sauce. Any remaining broth or liquor can be strained, cooled, and frozen in small batches for future use: it will be superb for gravy making!

The best accompaniment for this new way with beef is plenty of tiny Jersey potatoes tossed in butter and lightly sprinkled with nutmeg.

# *R*OAST FILLET (OR BONED LOIN) OF LAMB WITH LEEK SAUCE

*Serves 6*

*2 whole lamb fillets (weighing 12–14 oz (350–400 g) each)*

*2 oz (50 g) butter*

*1 level tsp salt*

*1 level tsp thyme*

*1 level tsp black pepper*

## SAUCE

*1 oz (25 g) butter*

*½ lb (225 g) young leeks, shredded*

*1 clove garlic, crushed*

*⅛ pint (75 ml) thin cream*

*2 tsp lemon juice*

*Salt only*

*⅛ pint (75 ml) cold water*

Preheat the oven to gas mark 9, 475°F (240°C). Make a paste with the butter, thyme, salt and pepper. Rub all over the lamb. Put the lamb into a small roasting tin and roast for 20–25 minutes. If you like your lamb less pink than this, continue the cooking time.

To make the sauce, melt the butter without colouring it. Add the leeks and garlic. Cover with a lid and soften the leeks over a low heat, stirring them from time to time to prevent colouring. Pass the leeks through a blender, then rub thugh a fine-meshed sieve. Transfer the sauce back to the pan, stir in the cream and lemon juice. Season carefully. Reheat, adding enough water to arrive at a pouring consistency. Serve the lamb carved into long, thin slices, with the sauce separately.

*Note*    Boned loin works very well with this recipe.

# $F$ILLET
## OF LAMB REFORM

*Serves 4–6*

$T$HIS dish, of course, is traditionally made with lamb cutlets, but if you consider how much is thrown away as bone and débris at the end of the meal, it is not really an extravagance to get rid of it all in the first place.

---

*2 × 10–12 oz (275–350 g) lamb fillet or boned loin, trimmed of all skin and fat*

*1 small egg, beaten with 2 tbsp water*

*4–6 oz (110–175 g) medium oatmeal*

*4 tbsp oil*

*4 oz (110 g) butter*

*Salt and milled pepper*

### $H$AM MOUSSE COATING

*6 oz (175 g) thick rasher of raw ham, cubed, including fat*

*1 small egg, beaten*

*¼ tsp ground mace*

*½ clove garlic, crushed*

*2 tbsp thick cream*

*Milled pepper*

## *Reform Sauce*

*12 fl oz (325 ml) tin of chicken consommé*

*2 fl oz (50 ml) red wine*

*1 oz (25 g) onion, finely chopped*

*4 fl oz (100 ml) tomato juice*

*2 tomatoes, skinned, deseeded and chopped*

*2 tsp red wine vinegar*

*1 heaped tsp redcurrant jelly*

## *To* GARNISH

*1 hard-boiled egg (white part only)*

*4 cocktail gherkins*

*1 oz (25 g) slice of tongue*

*1 level tbsp finely chopped parsley*

In a blender or food processor, first of all make a fine purée of all the ingredients for the ham mousse. You will not need to add salt, as the ham will be salty enough. Scrape the purée into a basin and put to stiffen for an hour or so in the refrigerator.

It is essential for the butcher, or for you, to trim off the silvery-blue skin on the lamb fillets. You will need a very sharp knife. Cut each one into 6 discs about 1¼–1½ inches (3–3.5 cm) thick. The pointed tail end of the fillets can be fried separately for lunch on another day. With the wetted butt of a rolling pin, very gently beat each disc – don't let it spread out more than ½ inch (1 cm) – and reform to shape. In a large frying pan, melt half the butter in 2 tablespoons of oil until it is lightly smoking. Seal the fillets for ½ minute on both sides. Season with salt and milled pepper. Leave to cool.

Spread a cushion of the ham mousse on each side of each fillet, making sure it is even. Put them on a kitchen tray and place in the refrigerator to firm. Dip each fillet in the beaten egg and roll in the oatmeal, patting the coating gently to fix it, and shake away any surplus. Melt the remaining butter with 2 tablespoons of oil until lightly smoking. Fry the fillets gently on each side for 1½–2 minutes, until golden-brown. Drain on crumpled kitchen paper.

Prepare the sauce just before serving. Have ready all the ingredients for the garnish, except the parsley, cut into matchstick-size striplets, or chopped finely. Bring the consommé, chopped onion and red wine to the boil and reduce, by boiling rapidly, to one good coffee-cup full. Add the tomato juice, chopped tomato, redcurrant jelly and vinegar. Boil for 2–3 minutes. Strain and rub the sauce through a fine sieve. Check the seasoning. Reheat, and add the garnish, allowing only enough time for this to heat through. Stir in the parsley. Serve 2 or 3 fillets per person, depending on how rich your first course was, and serve the sauce separately.

*Note*   This recipe can be made with the whole fillet. Split each one open by cutting in half lengthways almost all the way through. Open the fillets out, flatten them slightly, fill with the mousse, bring the halves together and tie at intervals with string. Coat with egg and oatmeal, and roast in ⅛ pint (75 ml) of smoking oil at gas mark 7, 425°F (220°C) for ½ to ¾ hour. Carve in oblique slices to serve.

# *B*RAISED VENISON WITH BLACKCURRANTS AND LIQUORICE

*Serves 4–5*

✦

*T*HE marriage of game with this very rich tangy sauce, which contains just a hint of liquorice, is perfect. Serve it with something quite plain to balance the richness of the dish.

*3–4 lb (1.4–1.8 kg) saddle of venison*

*1 leek*

*1 small onion*

*1 carrot*

*1 tsp tomato purée*

*1 tsp flour*

*2 oz (50 g) butter*

## *F*OR THE MARINADE

*4 oz (110 g) blackcurrants, plus 1 oz (25 g) for garnish*

*½ pint (275 ml) red wine*

*4 tbsp olive, grape-seed, or soy oil*

*1 clove garlic, crushed*

*2 sprigs fresh thyme*

*1 level tsp salt*

*20 to 30 twists of the pepper mill*

## FOR THE SAUCE

*¾ pint (400 ml) game stock (or use any good commercial game consommé)*

*2 tbsp port*

*2 tbsp blackcurrant or redcurrant jelly*

*1 tsp liquorice essence (optional)*

Have your butcher remove the top and under-fillets from the saddle (use the bones for the game stock on p. 21). Trim off all the fat and skin. You will have 2 large and 2 small pieces of meat. Put all the ingredients for the marinade into a large bowl. Add the venison pieces, cover with plastic film and leave for 5–6 hours. Take the pieces out, drain and pat them dry with paper kitchen towels.

Put all the used marinade ingredients plus the stock, or consommé, into a pan. Bring to the boil and reduce to ¾ pint (400 ml) by boiling rapidly. Strain, and put to one side.

Slice the leek, onion and carrot; fry them until golden-brown in 1 ounce (25 g) of the butter. Put into a roasting pan as a 'cushion' for the venison pieces. Dot the purée over and sprinkle with the flour. Melt the second ounce (25 g) of butter in a heavy-bottomed pan and seal the venison pieces on all sides over a high heat. Sit the pieces on top of the vegetables. Everything to this point can be done half a day in advance.

Preheat the oven to gas mark 9, 475°F (240°C). Roast the venison for 20–25 minutes; take out the 2 smaller fillets after 10–12 minutes (leave them longer if you prefer game well done). When the larger fillets are cooked remove them to a warm serving dish. Transfer the roasting pan to the top of the stove and fry the vegetables, stirring them well together for a minute or so. Pour over the strained, reduced marinade and cook, stirring for 3–4 minutes more. Add the blackcurrant or redcurrant jelly and ensure it melts. Strain the sauce into a clean pan and let it stand for 5 minutes. Skim off any excess fats which may have risen to the surface, using a small ladle or dessertspoon. Bring the sauce to the boil, and add the port (and liquorice if used).

Carve the venison into thin slices, allowing 2 pieces of top fillet per serving. Scatter a few whole blackcurrants onto each plate, spoon over a little of the rich sauce and arrange the venison slices on this.

Serve with pasta and a tossed salad.

*Note*  Essence of liquorice is available from dispensing chemists.

# $I$RISH STEW

*Serves 6*

$T$HE essential ingredients for a 'traditional' Irish stew are mutton (or lamb), onions, potatoes and parsley. I have added carrot and some diced bacon, and have upgraded the quality of the cut of lamb. All, I feel, in the Irish spirit, and I think you will enjoy the crunch of Irish scallions in the garnish.

*1 tbsp olive or soy oil*

*4 oz (110 g) fat bacon, diced*

*2 lamb fillets, approx. 1½ lb (700 g)*

*1 heaped tsp flour*

*1 small clove garlic, crushed*

*18 button onions, skinned*

*4 small carrots (10–12 oz: 275–350 g), cut into ½ inch (1 cm) dice*

*4 small new potatoes (12 oz: 350 g), cut into ½ inch (1 cm) dice*

*1 pint (570 ml) chicken stock*

*4 spring onions, with ½ inch (1 cm) of green left on, shredded*

*2 tbsp flat-leafed parsley, roughly chopped*

*2 medium (4 oz: 110 g) potatoes (see method)*

Preheat the oven to gas mark 5, 375°F (190°C). Trim the fat off the lamb and cut into ½ inch (1 cm) cubes. Heat the oil until smoking. Fry the bacon until lightly browned but not crisp. Transfer it with a slotted spoon to an 8 pint (4.5 litre) casserole. In the same oil, fry the cubes of lamb in 2 or 3 batches to seal and colour them lightly. Transfer to the casserole, discarding any excess fats. Sprinkle over the flour and stir well in. Add the onions, garlic and carrots. Cover with a pint (570 ml) of stock.

Cook in the oven for 1¼ hours, or until tender. Add the potatoes and continue cooking for a further 20 minutes, or until they are cooked. To acquire the true Irish Stew flavour, it is essential to have a little potato thickening without allowing the potatoes in the stew to go mushy, thus spoiling the overall texture. So, whilst the stew is cooking in the oven, have baking in their jackets alongside 2 medium-sized potatoes. Scoop out the soft inside and pass through a potato ricer or mash with a masher, adding a good knob of butter as you do so. Whisk enough of this into the stew for it to give it a light but definite thickness. Serve liberally sprinkled with the chopped parsley and spring onions.

# CURRIED LAMB WITH APPLE AND PINEAPPLE

*Serves 4*

| |
|---|
| *2 lb (900 g) fillet of leg of lamb (yields 1¼ lb: 550 g when boned and trimmed)* |
| *4 tbsp coconut oil* |
| *1 small onion, finely chopped* |
| *2 inch (5 cm) piece green ginger, peeled and finely sliced* |
| *1 clove garlic, crushed* |
| *2 heaped tsp mild curry powder* |
| *2 Cox's apples, peeled and cored* |
| *½ small pineapple, peeled and cored* |
| *1 oz (25 g) butter* |
| *Juice of 1 small lemon* |
| *Salt, pepper and mace* |
| *1 tsp sugar* |
| *¼ pint (150 ml) cream* |

Cut the lamb into ½ inch (1 cm) cubes. Heat the coconut oil until smoking and fry the lamb in batches to seal the meat on all sides, removing it to a plate with a slotted spoon when this is done. Add the onions to the pan and soften them in the residual fats. Return the meat to the pan, add the ginger, and continue cooking over a high heat until tender; the whole operation should take about 8–10 minutes, working over a good heat so that the meat is frying and not 'stewing'.

Meanwhile, cut the apples into quarters, then eighths; toss the pieces in the lemon juice. Cut the pineapple into pieces the same size. Melt 1 ounce (25 g) of butter until it is foaming, add the fruit, season with salt, pepper and mace, and the small amount of sugar. Add the lemon juice.

Stir the curry powder and garlic into the meat, and fry for a further minute, stirring all the time. Stir in the cream and bubble until it has cohered well. Add the apple and pineapple, which should be just cooked but still crisp. Reheat and serve with plain boiled rice.

# *L*ANCASHIRE HOT POTS

*Serves 6*

*I* WONDERED whether I was taking a severe liberty with this one: the result, I think, proves I was not!

*2 whole lamb fillets, trimmed and skinned*

*2 tbsp olive or soy oil for frying*

*24 button onions, skinned*

*3 inner stalks celery, finely diced*

*18 button mushrooms*

*Salt and milled pepper*

*¼ pint (150 ml) dry white wine, mixed with ¾ pint (400 ml) chicken stock*

*6 × 4 oz (110 g) potatoes, peeled and finely sliced*

*1 oz (25 g) melted butter*

*1 oz (25 g) pearl barley*

Have ready 6 ovenproof pots (approximately ⅔ pint (380 ml) size). Preheat the oven to gas mark 3, 325°F (170°C). Cut each fillet into 12 discs. Heat a little of the oil to smoking point. Quickly fry the lamb in small batches to seal and colour the meat. Place 4 pieces in each pot.

Brown the onions over a fairly fierce heat, adding a splash more oil if necessary. Lift them out with a draining spoon and divide between the pots. Do the same with the celery, mushrooms and pearl barley. A high heat and speed is best. Season the contents of each pot lightly with a dredge of salt and 2–3 twists of the pepper mill. Pour over enough wine and stock to cover. Arrange the finely sliced potatoes neatly in overlapping circles on top of each, and brush with melted butter. Season lightly with salt and pepper. Cook, lidded, in the preheated oven for 1½ hours. Take off the lids, raise the temperature to gas mark 5, 375°F (190°C) for a further 20–30 minutes, or until the potatoes are golden-brown.

*Note* If you make this as a single large hot pot, allow an extra 30 minutes' cooking time.

# *P*ORK FILLET WITH MUSTARD AND APPLES

*Serves 4*

*T*HIS recipe appears almost Chinese, yet all the ingredients have been used in the English repertory for centuries, often together.

*8 fl oz (225 ml) dry white wine or cider*

*1 pork fillet, 12–14 oz (350–400 g)*

*2 tbsp soy oil*

*1 good tsp dry mustard*

*1 clove garlic, crushed*

*2 pieces green ginger, peeled and sliced*

*2 oz (50 g) mushrooms, sliced*

*2 Cox's apples, peeled, cored and sliced*

*6 spring onions, cut into ½ inch (1 cm) pieces*

*Soy sauce*

*Salt and milled pepper*

Reduce the white wine or cider to half (4 fl oz: 100 ml) by boiling rapidly. Put on one side ready for use.

Cut the pork fillet in half lengthways and slice as thinly as possible. Cut it on the slant to give long, thin slivers – you should get 20–30 slices out of it. Heat the oil in a large frying pan until it is smoking well. Scatter in the pieces of pork fillet and work round with a spatula over a high heat until the meat is all sealed and has taken on a little colour. Scatter over the dry mustard, garlic and ginger: stir well in, and continue to fry, moving things about. Add the sliced apples and mushrooms. Splash over the soy sauce, pour in the wine and let everything bubble away whilst you stir and turn them. Season with salt and milled pepper.

When the juices are somewhat syrupy, add the spring onions and cook until they just wilt but are still crisp. If the sauce looks a little too reduced, add a spoonful of water. Serve with noodles, rice, pasta shells, etc.

# *R*OAST BONED LOIN OF PORK WITH TOMATO MADEIRA GRAVY

*Serves 4*

*4 ribs of pork in a piece, boned, rolled, well scored and tied*

*The bones from chining chopped into small pieces*

*1 bunch spring onions, trimmed and cut into 1 1/2 inch (3.5 cm) lengths*

*1 carrot, peeled and diced*

*1 tsp tomato purée*

*1/2 stock cube, crumbled*

*1 tsp dry mustard*

*1 sherry glass dry Madeira or Amontillado sherry*

*2 fl oz (50 ml) cold water*

*2 tomatoes, skinned and deseeded*

*2 fl oz (50 ml) tomato juice*

*Salt and milled pepper*

## *M*USTARD PASTE FOR THE CRACKLING

*2 oz (50 g) butter, softened and mixed with 1 tsp dry mustard*

*1 tsp salt*

*Milled pepper*

Preheat the oven to gas mark 8, 450°F (230°C). Butter or oil a roasting tin or ovenproof dish. Make a cushion in the bottom with the spring onions and carrots. Smear the tomato purée over this, and scatter with the mustard and the crumbled stock cube. Rub the mustard paste into the crackling and stand the loin on top of the bed of vegetables. Put the chine bones around. Roast in the preheated oven for 45 minutes to 1 hour.

Now remove the meat to a warm serving dish and cut away the strings. Stand the roasting pan on a medium to high flame, and brown the vegetables, scraping and moving them round with a wooden spatula. Pour in the Madeira or sherry and let it bubble well. If it ignites, don't worry – just let the flames die down. Add all the remaining ingredients and allow to bubble for 5 minutes until everything is amalgamated. Strain into a clean saucepan, and leave for 10 minutes to allow any excess fats to rise to the surface. Skim these off with a spoon and discard. Reheat the sauce, and serve with the pork carved in thin slices. (It helps if you remove the crackling and serve it separately.)

# SUGARED SPICED PORK CHOPS WITH APPLE AND WALNUTS

*Serves 4*

*4 thick pork chops, with the kidneys if possible*

*4 oz (110 g) muscovado sugar*

*2 tbsp cider vinegar, warmed*

*1 clove garlic, crushed*

*1 tsp dry mustard*

*2 fl oz (50 ml) olive or nut oil for frying*

*2 fl oz (50 ml) Amontillado sherry*

*2–3 oz (50–75 g) walnut halves*

*2 Cox's apples, peeled, and cut into 8 pieces*

*1 oz (25 g) butter*

*Salt, pepper*

*½ tsp ground cinnamon*

Nick the fat on the pork chops at ½ inch (1 cm) intervals. Using the tip of a wetted rolling pin, gently flatten the fat to only ¼ inch (0.5 cm) thick. Stir the sugar into the warm vinegar until dissolved. Stir in the mustard and garlic and pour into a shallow dish. Marinate the chops in this for an hour, turning them every now and then.

Heat the oil in a large heavy-bottomed pan until lightly smoking. Fry the pork chops in this for 4–5 minutes on each side, when they will be caramelised. Reduce the heat if the caramel shows signs of burning as opposed to browning! Remove the chops to a warm serving dish. Pour the sherry into the pan and allow to bubble for a minute. Strain and dribble this modicum of sauce over the chops.

In a second pan, melt the ounce (25 g) of butter until foaming. Toss the walnuts in this, add the apples and continue frying until the apples are hot, golden, but still firmish. Season well with salt, pepper and a dredge of cinnamon. Arrange around the chops on a serving dish.

# *H*AM AND CHICKEN CREAMS WRAPPED IN LETTUCE LEAVES WITH SCALLION SAUCE

*Serves 4–6*

*6 oz (175 g) raw chicken breast*

*6 oz (175 g) raw lean gammon*

*2 eggs, beaten*

*1/4 tsp ground nutmeg*

*1 level tsp salt*

*1 level tsp finely grated lemon zest*

*1/2 tsp milled white pepper or 1/4 tsp ground ginger*

*5 fl oz (150 ml) double cream*

*24 lettuce, or Chinese cabbage leaves*

*Chicken stock (use carcass or stock cube)*

## *F*OR THE SAUCE

*2 large egg yolks*

*4 oz (110 g) butter, melted and hot*

*Juice of 1 lemon*

*1 tbsp water*

*1/4 tsp salt*

*2 fl oz (50 ml) double cream, warmed*

*6 spring onions (scallions), washed and finely shredded*

Make a fine purée of the ham and chicken meat in a food processor, with the beaten eggs, adding all the seasonings. Scrape the mixture into a bowl and beat in the cream. Chill well (overnight or all day).

Wash the Chinese leaves or lettuce. Bring a pan of lightly salted water to the boil. Blanch the leaves for 30 seconds, a few at a time. Rinse under cold water and pat dry. Arrange 2 leaves in a cross. Put a dessertspoonful of the purée in the centre. Wrap the stalk ends over first, then the green ends over on top, and tie with fine string or linen thread. Poach them, barely covered by the simmering stock, in a shallow pan for 15–20 minutes. Drain. Remove string; they will keep warm for 20 minutes or so in a warm dish in the oven at gas mark 1, 275°F (140°C) if they are covered with a clean, damp napkin wrung out in scalding water, while you are making the sauce. Mix the egg yolks, salt, lemon juice and water in a pyrex bowl. Stand the bowl over a pan of boiling water and whisk gently until it thickens. Remove the basin from the heat. Dribble in the hot melted butter, whisking hard and allowing the emulsion to thicken as you go along. Stir in the cream. Add the raw onions just before serving. Do not reheat.

# Glazed ham, chicken and brie pasty with watercress

*Serves 4*

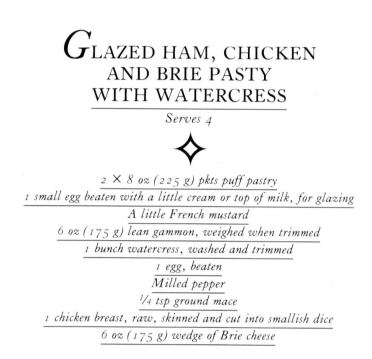

*2 × 8 oz (225 g) pkts puff pastry*

*1 small egg beaten with a little cream or top of milk, for glazing*

*A little French mustard*

*6 oz (175 g) lean gammon, weighed when trimmed*

*1 bunch watercress, washed and trimmed*

*1 egg, beaten*

*Milled pepper*

*¼ tsp ground mace*

*1 chicken breast, raw, skinned and cut into smallish dice*

*6 oz (175 g) wedge of Brie cheese*

Preheat the oven to gas mark 7, 425°F (220°C). Roll out the first packet of pastry to a square approximately 10 × 10 inches (25.5 × 25.5 cm). Spread thinly with mustard to within an inch (2.5 cm) of the edge all round. In a food processor make a purée of the gammon and watercress, using the beaten egg as liquid. Turn into a bowl. Season with milled pepper and mace (it won't need any salt). Mix in the chicken pieces.

Arrange thin slices of the cheese over the pastry to within an inch (2.5 cm) of the edge. Pile the ham mixture on this, making it level. Fold up the inch edge of pastry. Brush with the egg glaze.

Roll out the second packet of pastry to the same size and fit on top. Brush with egg glaze all over, and put to chill for 30 minutes. Brush all over again with the beaten egg. Make a pattern with a knife but be careful not to cut right through the pastry. Brush again with the remaining egg and cream glaze: it will give the pastry a lovely golden colour. Bake for 20 minutes, then lower the heat to gas mark 5, 375°F (190°C) for a further 20 minutes. Cut into 4 when cooled.

# CREAMED KIDNEYS WITH APPLES

*Serves 4*

*I*F you have never been an offal lover, this may be the recipe that converts you.

*2 pigs' kidneys, skinned and trimmed of all fat*

*2 tbsp soy oil*

*¼ tsp ground cinnamon*

*Salt and milled pepper*

*2 Cox's apples, peeled, cored, quartered and sliced*

*4 spring onions, trimmed and cut diagonally into ½ inch (1 cm) pieces*

*2 fl oz (50 ml) Amontillado sherry or dry cider*

*¼ pint (150 ml) single cream*

*4 crisp buttered toasts, with the crusts off, or
2 split muffins toasted on both sides*

Cut each kidney into the thinnest possible slices – you should get 10–12 from each kidney! Heat the oil in a large frying pan until it is smoking well. Scatter the slices of kidney in the oil, and fry over a brisk heat for 3–4 minutes, stirring them well round with a wooden spatula. Season with salt, pepper and the modest amount of cinnamon. Lower the heat, add the onions and apples, and continue frying until they are softened. Add the sherry and let it bubble for a few seconds before adding the cream. Stir well together until all has cohered. If the sauce looks oily, add a spoonful of stock or water and bring back to the boil, stirring everything well in. Spoon on to the hot toasts or muffins.

# CALVES' LIVER WITH PINK GRAPEFRUIT

*Serves 4*

*8 × 2 oz (50 g) slivers of calves' liver*
*1 tsp each of salt, milled pepper and ground coriander*
*2 oz (50 g) butter*
*2 tbsp oil*
*2 pink grapefruits, knife-segmented*
*1 small glass (1 fl oz: 25 ml) whisky or brandy*
*1 tbsp snipped chives*
*1 tbsp roughly chopped flat-leafed parsley or fresh coriander leaves*

Mix the three seasonings together in a cup. Melt 1 oz (25 g) butter and the oil in a large frying pan until it is lightly smoking. Lower in the slivers of liver, making sure they are away from you so that you don't splash your hands. Fry over a good strong heat, seasoning lightly as you go along. Turn the pieces over, and fry on the second side, seasoning this as well. Allow 1½–2 minutes per side, depending on how well cooked you like liver. Continue frying and turning the liver for another minute or two. Remove to a warm serving dish.

Return the pan to the heat, pour in the whisky or brandy, add a further ounce (25 g) of butter and the grapefruit segments. Season them lightly. Allow them to heat through without breaking up. Garnish each piece of liver with a few grapefruit segments. Strain over the juices, sprinkle with the fresh herbs, and serve.

# CALVES' LIVER WITH SHERRY VINEGAR, ONIONS AND MUSHROOMS

*Serves 4*

THESE days, many kinds of vinegar are widely available from supermarkets and delicatessens, and this recipe makes good use of one of the more unusual ones.

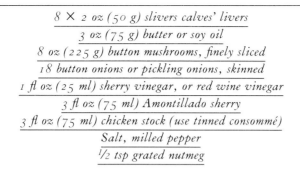

8 × 2 oz (50 g) slivers calves' livers

3 oz (75 g) butter or soy oil

8 oz (225 g) button mushrooms, finely sliced

18 button onions or pickling onions, skinned

1 fl oz (25 ml) sherry vinegar, or red wine vinegar

3 fl oz (75 ml) Amontillado sherry

3 fl oz (75 ml) chicken stock (use tinned consommé)

Salt, milled pepper

1/2 tsp grated nutmeg

Part boil the onions for 2–3 minutes. Drain well.

Melt 2 ounces (50 g) of the butter in a large frying pan. Fry the liver in two batches – about 1 minute on each side, depending on how thin the liver is and how well done you like it. Season lightly and remove the liver to a warm serving dish. Add the extra ounce (25 g) of butter to the pan and swirl it round. Fry the onions to colour them, adding the mushrooms after a minute or so. Season with salt, pepper and nutmeg. Take the pan from the heat whilst you remove the mushrooms and onions with a slotted spoon, and spoon them over the liver. Return the pan to a moderate heat. Add the vinegar, and scrape all the sediments together as it bubbles and reduces. Add the sherry and stock and reduce to about 2 tablespoonfuls of strong sauce. Dribble this evenly over the liver.

# $P$AN-FRIED VEAL WITH SAGE LEAVES, APRICOTS AND CREAM

*Serves 4*

4 escalopes of veal, each weighing 4–5 oz (110–150 g)

2 tbsp olive oil

2 oz (50 g) butter

Salt and milled pepper

2 fl oz (50 ml) light rum

8 apricots, fresh, tinned or dried (soaked in the rum)

12 sage leaves, finely shredded

1/4 pint (150 ml) single cream

Flatten the escalopes gently with the butt of a wetted rolling pin to prevent the flesh dragging. If using fresh apricots, halve and stone them.

Heat half the oil and butter until foaming and just turning brown. Over a high heat brown and fry 2 escalopes of veal for 1–2 minutes on each side. Remove to a warm serving dish. Repeat the process, adding more butter and oil to the pan if necessary. Season lightly with salt and pepper as you go along.

Add the rum to the hot pan – it will ignite. Pour in the cream to quell the flames, reduce the heat, add the sage and apricots, and simmer until the fruit is tender and the sauce has cohered. If the sauce looks oily at the edges, add a spoonful of water. Spoon over the escalopes.

# COLD PUDDINGS AND ICES

*I never advocate an over-indulgence of sweet puddings. I do, however, believe that a treat, once in a while, is good for us. If you decide to serve that treat at the end of an excellent meal, then it should be delicately prepared from the richest ingredients: thick cream, unsalted butter with its unsurpassed flavour, bitter chocolate, aromatic liqueurs, farm eggs, flower-toned honey and fresh fruits.* ◆ *You cannot go wrong if you remember that small is beautiful; where at one time large portions were the order of the day, today even the pudding-loving British are happy with delicate spoonfuls of luscious mousses and home-made ices to round off a perfect meal.*

# *R*ICH RICE PUDDING

*Serves 6–8*

◆

*A*LL the ingredients of a traditional eighteenth-century rice pudding are here brought back together again and enriched with cream. I like it best served cold, studded with candied or crystallised fruits. The subtle complement of an extra spoonful of *unsweetened* thick chilled cream is worth breaking the diet rules for.

*1 pint (570 ml) milk*
*3 oz (75 g) Carolina (pudding) rice, washed*
*2 oz (50 g) caster sugar (or less)*
*¼ tsp grated nutmeg*
*1 tsp lemon zest*
*1 tsp pure vanilla essence (or pod)*
*2 oz (50 g) candied orange, finely diced, soaked overnight in 2 tbsp whisky*
*1 pint (570 ml) double or whipping cream (see method)*
*2 large egg yolks (if served hot)*
*1 level tsp gelatine crystals dissolved in 2 tbsp cold water (if served cold)*
*Other candied or fresh fruits for garnish*

Put the milk, rice, sugar, vanilla, lemon zest and nutmeg into a lidded double boiler. Boil until the rice is completely soft (about 45 minutes).

## *T*O SERVE HOT

Stir in the candied fruit, unwhipped cream, and the 2 egg yolks. Transfer the pudding to a buttered 3–4 inch (7.5–10 cm) deep dish. Stand this in a water bath and bake at gas mark 6, 400°F (200°C) for 20 minutes until the traditional skin has formed. Serve with raspberry cullis (see p. 196).

## *T*O SERVE COLD

While the cooked rice is still hot stir the gelatine in thoroughly. Leave to cool. Gradually incorporate the candied fruit and the cream, which should be half-whipped to ribbon stage. Chill, covered with plastic film. Serve in a glass bowl garnished with extra candied fruits or flaked almonds. (The mixture will thicken somewhat as it chills.)

# *E*TON MESS

*Serves 6*

*T*HIS traditional mishmash of strawberries, cream and meringues is said to have emanated from Eton College, no doubt because the boys could rustle it up in the 'dorm'. It becomes an elegant dinner-party dessert when made like this. The only sugar is in the meringues, though you can add a little to the raspberries if you so wish.

*8 oz (225 g) raspberries*
*1 tbsp cold water*
*1 lb (450 g) strawberries, quartered*
*¼ pint (150 ml) double cream*
*¼ pint (150 ml) natural yoghurt*
*4 meringue shells, finely crushed*
*6 even-sized strawberries, for garnish*

Toss the raspberries with the water in a pan over a low heat until the juices draw and the fruit begins to fall. Leave to cool, then rub and press the purée through a fine sieve. Arrange the quartered or sliced strawberries in the bottom of a glass bowl and spoon the purée over.

Mix the cream and yoghurt together and whip until the mixture reaches the soft peak stage. Spread it over the strawberries and level the top, using the edge of a plastic spatula. Scatter a cushion of the crushed meringue over the cream and garnish with the strawberries. Shape into fans by making four or five incisions in each strawberry, ending each cut ¼ inch (0.5 cm) from the stalk end; fan the pieces out by pressing gently with your finger.

# *E*IGHTEENTH-CENTURY ALMOND CHEESECAKES

*Makes 16–20 tartlets*

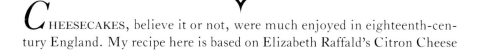

*C*HEESECAKES, believe it or not, were much enjoyed in eighteenth-century England. My recipe here is based on Elizabeth Raffald's Citron Cheese

Cakes. Instead of the more usual 'puff-paste', I have lined the tins with 'finger-tip' pastry.

## PASTRY

*6 oz (175 g) plain white flour, sieved with*
*3 oz (75 g) ground almonds*
*3 oz (75 g) caster sugar*
*1 tsp grated orange rind*
*1 egg (size 4)*
*3 oz (75 g) chilled butter, cut into bits*
*Orange jelly marmalade or sieved apricot jam*

## ALMOND CHEESE FILLING

*3 oz (75 g) unsalted butter, softened*
*5 oz (150 g) caster sugar*
*2 whole eggs, beaten*
*5 oz (150 g) ground almonds, sieved on to a paper*
*1 oz (25 g) plain white flour sieved with the ground almonds*
*1 tsp finely grated orange zest*
*1 tbsp triple-strength orange flower water*

## TO GARNISH

*2 oz (50 g) flaked almonds*
*8 strips glacé (not candied) orange or mandarin (optional)*

Preheat the oven to gas mark 6, 400°F (200°C). Brush some tartlet tins with clarified unsalted butter. I make the pastry by the all-in-one method in a food processor. Roll out the pastry thinly. Cut circles ¼ inch (0.5 cm) larger than the diameter of the tins. Line them and bake blind in the preheated oven for 15–20 minutes. Cool. Put a teaspoon of orange jelly marmalade or sieved apricot jam into the base of each baked tartlet. Spread it evenly or it may bubble up through the almond mixture.

Cream the butter and sugar for the filling until light and fluffy. Beat in the eggs, and mix in the flower water and orange zest. Cut and fold in the sieved ground almonds and flour. Spoon the mixture into the tartlets and

*Page 171 Boiled Fillet of Beef and Caper Sauce*
*Page 172 Roast Loin of Lamb with Leek Sauce*

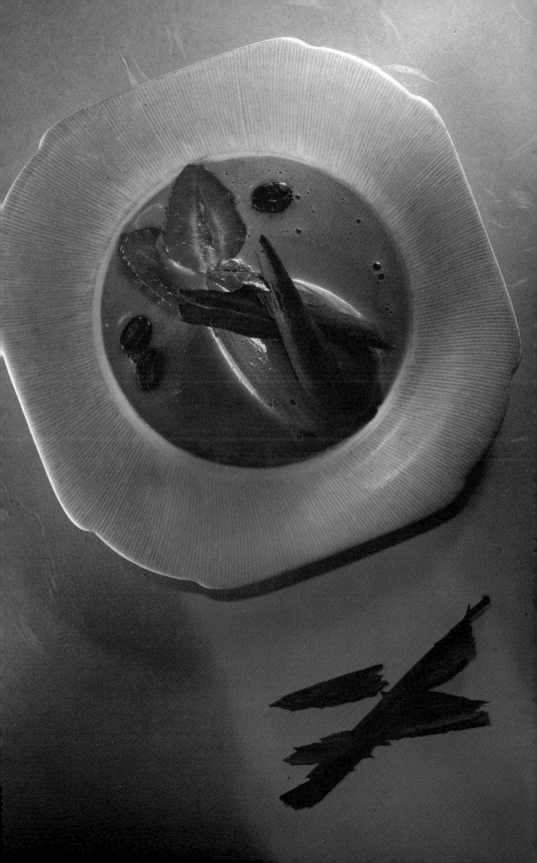

level the tops. Sprinkle with flaked almonds and pop a piece of glacé fruit in the centre of each. Bake at gas mark 4, 350°F (180°C) for 20 minutes, lowering the temperature to gas mark 3, 325°F (170°C) for 10 minutes.

# Coconut whisky roll

*Serves 6–8*

## Sponge Mixture

*4 large eggs*
*4 oz (110 g) caster sugar*
*3 oz (75 g) S.R. flour, sieved*
*1 oz (25 g) toasted desiccated coconut (see below)*

## Whisky cream filling

*6 large egg yolks*
*1 1/2 oz (40 g) caster sugar*
*1/2 pint (275 ml) single cream*
*1/2 sachet gelatine crystals*
*3 oz (75 g) unsalted butter, creamed*
*3 fl oz (75 ml) whisky*

## Topping

*1/3 pint (190 ml) double cream*
*2 tbsp whisky*
*1 dsp caster sugar*
*Extra toasted coconut*
*Pieces of glacé (or fresh) pineapple, or other candied or glacé fruits*

Preheat the oven to gas mark 5, 375°F (190°C).

Have ready a buttered and butter-papered 14 × 9 inch (35.5 × 23 cm) swiss roll tin and a clean tea-cloth wrung out in cold water laid on a flat surface. Cover this with a piece of greaseproof paper (at least 18 × 12 inches:

*Page 173 Chocolate Mousse with Coffee Sauce    Page 174 Jellied Fresh Blackcurrants*

45.5 × 30.5 cm), and dredge it evenly with caster sugar. Using a rotary or electric hand whisk, cream the eggs and sugar until the whisk leaves a very distinct trail when drawn through the mixture. Mix the toasted coconut and flour thoroughly, and then deftly cut and fold into the egg mixture. Pour into the lined tray and bake in the preheated oven for 12 minutes. Invert onto the prepared paper for 2 minutes, then carefully remove the base paper. Leave for ½ minute to allow steam to escape. Now ease and gradually roll the cake up very carefully, and quite loosely, using the damp cloth to help you. Unroll it, and re-roll loosely in the paper only. Leave to cool.

You should have the filling already prepared. In a round-bottomed basin arranged over a pan of *boiling* water, slowly whisk the egg yolks, sugar, cream and gelatine until thick and 'ribboning'. Remove from the heat and pour the whisky in immediately to remove any residual heat. Arrange the bowl or pan in a sink of cold water, whisking to cool it a little and, at the same time, whisking in the softened butter bit by bit. Cool, then chill it, covered with plastic film. Whisk it from time to time to make sure you get a thick, even-textured mixture — you should be able to spread it easily. If it appears too thick add a little more whisky or single cream.

Now unroll the sponge again. Spread the cream filling to the edges and dredge with extra toasted coconut. Re-roll. Whip the first three of the topping ingredients to a piping consistency. Pipe a garland down the centre of the roll. Dredge with more toasted coconut and spike with glacé fruit. This confection ought to be eaten the day it is made, though it will freeze.

### TO TOAST THE COCONUT

Preheat the oven to gas mark 6, 400°F (200°C). Spread 6 ounces (175 g) of desiccated coconut on an oven tray. Using the 'blade' edge of a palette knife, gather up and respread the coconut at regular intervals (every 2 minutes, once the edges start to turn light gold). When evenly browned and *dry*, turn on to a clean tray or paper to cool.

# LEMON TARTS

*Serves 6*

*8 oz (225 g) rich shortcrust pastry (p. 217)*

## LEMON CREAM FILLING

*2 oz (50 g) unsalted butter*

*½ cup lemon juice*

*1 tbsp grated lemon zest (4 lemons)*

*12 oz (350 g) caster sugar*

*5 eggs, beaten*

Roll out the pastry to line six 4 inch (10 cm) pastry pans. Bake blind until brown and crisp. In a double boiler (not aluminium as this discolours the mixture), or in a basin over a pan of boiling water, heat the butter, lemon juice and rind with the sugar until it has completely dissolved and is very hot. Remove the liner from the heat and whisk in the beaten eggs at a slow dribble. The mixture will thicken: if not, return the liner to the pan of boiling water and whisk gently until it does. Cool, then chill well. Spread the lemon mixture into the crisp tart cases. Pipe a blob of cream on the top and serve.

# *T*RIPLE CREAM PUDDING

*Serves 8–10*

*I* HAVE for a long time thought that I would like to create a dish that married England's three 'creams', though it be a *ménage à trois*! Here is the result of my testing and tasting – probably the richest sweet you will ever serve, it has to be for a very high-flown occasion.

## *C*USTARD CREAM

*4 whole eggs*

*2 extra egg yolks*

*1 piece vanilla pod*

*½ pint (275 ml) milk*

*½ pint (275 ml) single cream*

*1½–2 oz (40–50 g) caster sugar*

*12 apricots, freshly stewed or tinned*

## *E*NGLISH BURN'T CREAM

*8 egg yolks*

*2 oz ( 50 g) caster sugar*

*1 pint ( 570 ml) single cream*

*1 sachet gelatine crystals*


## *C*ARAMEL LAYER

*4 oz ( 1 1 0 g) caster sugar*

*⅛ pint ( 75 ml) water*


## *T*O GARNISH

*16 fl oz ( 425 ml) clotted cream*


Infuse the milk, cream, sugar and vanilla pod in a pan over a low heat for 10 minutes. Remove the pod. Beat the whole eggs well. Pour on the hot mixture and strain into a fireproof dish. Bake in a water bath at gas mark 2, 300°F (150°C) for 1–1½ hours, or until set. Wipe the sides of the dish and leave to cool.

Drain the apricots, and purée by pressing through a fine sieve after blending. Spoon the purée over the cooled custard.

Make the Burn't Cream. Beat the egg yolks and sugar until light and fluffy. Bring the cream to the boil. Pour the egg mixture over, and return the pan to minimal heat. Using a small balloon whisk, stir until it is as thick as double cream. Plunge the bottom of the pan into a sink of cold water to remove any residual heat. Melt the gelatine in a teacup with 1 tablespoon of water. Stand the cup in a small pan of simmering water to make sure it is completely dissolved. Whisk the melted gelatine well into the cream. Cool until it is beginning to gel. *Ladle* the mixture carefully over the custard and apricot purée. Put in the refrigerator to set.

In an aluminium pan (some enamels are affected by excessive heat) bring the water and the sugar to the boil for the caramel layer and continue boiling until a good rich caramel is arrived at. Stand the pan on a heatproof mat and either pour or ladle a caramel coating on top of the set cream. Start in the centre and spiral outwards.

Just before serving, dip a teaspoon into boiling water, quickly drying it each time, and scoop out oval shapes of the clotted cream and drop these on top of the caramel.

# RUM CUSTARDS

*Serves 8*

*1¼ pints (700 ml) milk*
*¼ pint (150 ml) single cream*
*3 whole eggs*
*3 extra egg yolks*
*2–3 oz (50–75 g) caster sugar*
*½ tsp vanilla essence*
*2 tbsp Bacardi or other light rum*

Whisk the whole eggs and the yolks with the sugar without overworking them. Bring the milk and cream to the boil. Add the vanilla essence and rum. Pour the hot mixture over the eggs, whisking well in. Strain through a fine sieve back into the pan or into a jug. Pour into individual custard pots or ramekins and stand these in a deep ovenproof dish or tin filled two-thirds full with hot water. Cook at gas mark 4, 350°F (180°C) for 12–15 minutes, until just set. Cool, then chill. Serve decorated with a blob of whipped cream.

# BURN'T CREAMS WITH GINGER AND RASPBERRIES

*Serves 6*

*B*URN'T Cream must be included in any self-respecting book on English cookery. This dish is best made as individual puddings in small fireproof ramekins.

*2 whole eggs and 2 egg yolks*
*½ pint (275 ml) single cream*
*1 oz (25 g) caster sugar*
*1 large piece stem ginger, finely chopped*
*1 level tsp gelatine crystals dissolved in 1 tbsp boiling water*
*4 oz (110 g) fresh or defrosted frozen raspberries*
*Icing sugar for glazed topping*

## TO GARNISH

*1 extra piece stem ginger, sliced into 6*
*Whipped cream (optional)*

Beat the whole eggs and egg yolks. Bring the cream, sugar and chopped ginger to the boil, pour over the eggs, whisking all the time. Mix in the small amount of melted gelatine. Divide the raspberries evenly between 6 ramekins. Pour over the cream mixture and leave to cool and set.

Preheat the grill to spanking hot. Dredge the top of the creams with a good ⅛ inch (0.25 cm) cushion of icing sugar. Wipe the edges clean. Stand the ramekins in a tin of ice-cold water, slide this under the grill and let the sugar melt to a good dark caramel colour. Cool, but do not refrigerate again as this will soften the crisp layer of caramel. Decorate with a slice of stem ginger and/or a blob of whipped cream.

# *R*ATAFIA TRIFLE

*Serves 6*

*T*HIS is undoubtedly England's most excellent sweet. Over the years I have complained as fruit (tinned at that), jelly (always a packet one) and artificial custards have crept into the recipe. The essential ingredients are the ratafia biscuit, rich English custard, wine and cream; this latter ideally in the form of a syllabub. The sponge cake has to be 'without butter', as Elizabeth Raffald tells us in her *The Experienced English Housekeeper* of 1769.

*3 trifle biscuits, crumbled*
*6 good tsp rich Madeira or cream sherry*

## CUSTARD

*½ pint (275 ml) single cream*
*4 egg yolks*
*1 oz (25 g) vanilla sugar or 1 oz (25 g) sugar and 1 tsp vanilla essence*
*¼ tsp gelatine crystals*
*4 oz (110 g) ratafia biscuits, roughly but evenly crushed*

## APRICOT PURÉE

*3 tbsp good quality apricot jam*

*4 apricot caps, fresh or tinned, roughly cut up*

*3 tbsp water*

## SYLLABUB

*½ pint (275 ml) double cream*

*⅛ pint (75 ml) Madeira or cream sherry*

*1 oz (25 g) caster sugar*

*Juice and grated zest of 1 small orange*

## TO GARNISH

*18 small ratafia biscuits*

*6 crystallised violets or other flowers*

Prepare the custard by creaming the egg yolks and sugar together, with the vanilla essence if used. Bring the cream to the boil, and sprinkle over the modest amount of gelatine crystals, whisking away from the heat until dissolved. Pour the hot liquid over the egg yolk mixture, whisking well. Return the pan to a low heat and stir with a wooden spoon until a clean trail is left when the finger is drawn over the back of the spoon. Leave to cool. Bring the ingredients for the purée to the boil, and simmer until sticky (about 2–3 minutes). Cool and press through a fine-meshed wire sieve. Make the syllabub in a glass bowl, using a balloon whisk to incorporate and whisk all the ingredients together until the cream stands in firm peaks.

When ready to assemble the trifle, crumble the sponge fingers into a bowl and splash with enough of the wine to moisten them without making them soggy. Divide the crumbs between six 6 ounce (175 g) glasses. Spoon over the chilled custard, then a cushion of the crisp ratafias. Spoon over a dessertspoonful of the apricot purée. Using a broad nozzle fitted into a pastry bag, pipe over the syllabub. Finally, decorate with three ratafias and one crystallised flower to each.

# CHOCOLATE SPONGE TURNOVERS

*Serves 6*

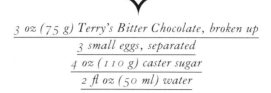

3 oz (75 g) Terry's Bitter Chocolate, broken up

3 small eggs, separated

4 oz (110 g) caster sugar

2 fl oz (50 ml) water

## FOR THE FILLING

¾ pint (400 ml) whipping cream

2 tsp icing sugar

1 tsp vanilla essence

2–3 oz (50–75 g) bitter chocolate, grated or crushed

Icing sugar for dredging

Preheat the oven to gas mark 5, 375°F (190°C).

Have ready two baking sheets lined with silicone paper. Put the broken chocolate with the water in a basin and arrange this over a pan of boiling water to melt. Cream the yolks and sugar until light and fluffy, and whisk the egg whites until they stand in firm peaks. Using a spatula, scrape the warm melted chocolate into the egg mixture, and cut and mix in the beaten whites.

Spoon approximately 2 fluid ounces (50 ml) or 2 tablespoons of the mixture onto the prepared baking sheets, and, with a palette knife, spread it evenly into 12 circles approximately 4 inches (10 cm) in diameter. Bake in the oven for 10–12 minutes. Remove, and leave the sponge circles on the sheet, covered with a damp cloth or piece of greaseproof paper wrung out in cold water. This is to prevent a sugary crust forming which would inhibit the rolling or folding of the circles. Leave to cool.

Whip the cream for the filling with the sugar and vanilla essence until it stands in soft peaks. Fold in the crushed chocolate and continue whipping until the mixture is just firm and easily spread. Divide the cream between the 12 sponge circles; fold them over, and serve dredged with icing sugar.

# CHOCOLATE MOUSSE WITH COFFEE SAUCE

*Serves 6–8*

*T*HIS is a very, very rich mousse, velvety in texture, so a little goes a long way!

*1 whole egg and 1 egg yolk*

*2 × 3½ oz (85 g) blocks Terry's Bitter Chocolate*

*2 tbsp crème de cacao*

*1 tbsp brandy*

*12 fl oz (325 ml) cream, half double and half single*

## COFFEE SAUCE

*6 egg yolks*

*¼ pint (150 ml) coffee, made with Continental Blend*

*3 tbsp sugar*

*2 tbsp coffee liqueur or brandy*

*¼ pint (150 ml) single cream*

Melt the chocolate in a bowl over boiling water. Whisk the egg and egg yolk in a second bowl over a pan of simmering water until it has a thick, custard-like texture. Cool, but do not allow to set, so keep whisking gently from time to time, using a balloon whisk.

Lightly whip the cream with the liqueurs to the soft peak stage. Fold the melted chocolate into the eggs, making sure they are about the same temperature. Finally, fold in the whipped cream. Pour into a bowl and leave to set in the refrigerator for about 4 hours, covered with plastic film.

Make the sauce. Whisk the yolks, sugar and coffee in a bowl over hot water until it becomes quite thick and the yolks are cooked. Then mix in the cream and your chosen liqueur. Cool, then chill.

To serve this attractively, use a spoon dipped into boiling water to spoon out the mousse into egg shapes and place on a lake of the chilled coffee sauce.

# CRANACHAN

*Serves 6*

JANE Grigson in her book *British Cookery* rightly acclaims Scottish raspberries as the best in Europe: I endorse that, and recommend them for use in this dish which is ideally suited to today's scheme of things.

| |
|---|
| *3 oz (75 g) coarse oatmeal, toasted and cooled* |
| *¹/₂ pint (275 ml) double cream* |
| *1–2 oz (25–50 g) caster sugar* |
| *2 fl oz (50 ml) malt whisky* |
| *8 oz (225 g) small raspberries* |

Whip the cream with the sugar and whisky until it stands in fairly soft peaks. Gently cut and mix in the toasted oatmeal, then spoon the mixture into glasses, layering with the raspberries as you go along. An alternative way to make this simple but delicious sweet is to put all the raspberries into a glass bowl, spoon over all the cream, and finish with a final layer of toasted oatmeal.

# ATHOL BROSE

*Serves 6*

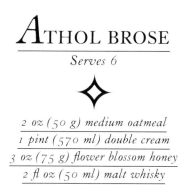

| |
|---|
| *2 oz (50 g) medium oatmeal* |
| *1 pint (570 ml) double cream* |
| *3 oz (75 g) flower blossom honey* |
| *2 fl oz (50 ml) malt whisky* |

Scatter the oatmeal evenly on a meticulously clean baking sheet. Toast in the oven, gas mark 6, 400°F (200°C) until golden-brown, spreading and rescattering the oatmeal with a wooden spatula every 2 minutes. (The procedure will take 10–15 minutes.) Cool.

Now whisk the cream with the honey and whisky until it reaches the soft peak stage. (This is usually better and more safely done with a hand or rotary whisk.) Gently mix in the cold crisp oatmeal, reserving a little for the top. Spoon the mixture into individual glasses and cover each with plastic film before chilling. It will thicken slightly as it chills, so avoid over-peaking at the whipping stage so that the cream remains 'spoonable'.

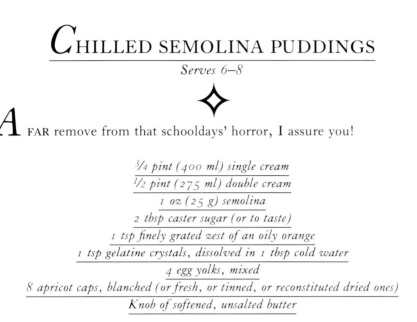

# *C*HILLED SEMOLINA PUDDINGS

*Serves 6–8*

*A* FAR remove from that schooldays' horror, I assure you!

*³/₄ pint (400 ml) single cream*
*¹/₂ pint (275 ml) double cream*
*1 oz (25 g) semolina*
*2 tbsp caster sugar (or to taste)*
*1 tsp finely grated zest of an oily orange*
*1 tsp gelatine crystals, dissolved in 1 tbsp cold water*
*4 egg yolks, mixed*
*8 apricot caps, blanched (or fresh, or tinned, or reconstituted dried ones)*
*Knob of softened, unsalted butter*

### APRICOT SAUCE

*³/₄ lb (350 g) fresh or drained tinned apricots, pitted*
*Sugar, if needed*
*1 tbsp lemon juice*
*1 tbsp apricot liqueur or Grand Marnier*

In a non-stick pan bring the single cream, sugar and zest slowly to the boil, rain in the semolina, reduce the heat and simmer for 3–4 minutes. Remove from the heat and, whilst still hot, mix the softened gelatine and the egg yolks in well. Cool. Whip the double cream just to the ribbon stage and cut into the mixture.

Have ready 8 lightly buttered individual moulds (use coffee cups if you don't have a set of tin ones). Put an apricot cap in the bottom of each, curved side down. Fill with the semolina mixture. Chill.

Purée the apricots for the sauce in a blender or food processor, and then rub through a fine-meshed sieve. Add the remaining ingredients and chill.

Turn the semolina puddings out of the moulds by easing the edge with your finger. Dip each tin for a couple of seconds into a basin of boiling water and wipe dry. Turn on to individual plates in a pond of apricot sauce.

# $B$LANCMANGE

*Serves 8*

*L*ITERALLY the name means 'white food', and for centuries this is precisely what it was – usually a potage based on white fish or capon breast. In the eighteenth century almonds made an appearance in the recipes and the dish was served, porridge-like in texture, sprinkled with sugar. Just how, or even exactly when, in the nineteenth century the name became attached to the travesty of a mould composed solely of cornflour and milk we remember with horror from the nursery is difficult to trace, but to mention the word 'blancmange' in recent years has been enough to arouse ridicule. Here I have not so much up-marketed the recipe as returned to the pages of the master cooks of the eighteenth century, whose receipts for blancmange are not dissimilar to what we know as Bavarian Cream.

*2 tsp gelatine crystals*

*1 tbsp cold water*

*4 large egg yolks*

*4 oz (110 g) caster sugar*

*1/2 pint (275 ml) single cream*

*1/2 pint (275 ml) double cream whipped to soft peak*

*2 oz (50 g) toasted ground almonds*

*1 oz (25 g) toasted flaked almonds for an optional garnish*

Stand a cup containing the gelatine and water in a pan of simmering water: stir occasionally to ensure the gelatine is fully melted. Cream the egg yolks and sugar in a pyrex bowl until light and fluffy. Bring the single cream to the boil and pour over the egg mixture, whisking to ensure all is well mixed. Return the pan to a low heat, exchange the whisk for a wooden straight-edged spatula and, stirring all the time (using the straight edge to prevent the mixture on the bottom of the pan from clotting), let it thicken until a distinct trail is left when the finger is drawn across the back of the spatula. Whisk in the melted gelatine thoroughly, using a balloon whisk.

Cool until almost setting. Mix in the toasted almonds, then cut and fold in the whipped cream. Spoon into individual cups. Put to set (it will be a 'soft' set). Serve simply garnished with a few toasted flaked almonds.

# SUMMER PUDDING

*Serves 6–8*

*T*HE temptation to use cake in place of the traditional bread was difficult to resist, but I settle instead for a two days' old, top-quality white Jewish bread. Made in an oblong mould or loaf tin, I serve this new version of an old favourite cut into ¾ inch (1.5 cm) slices and topped with rich pouring cream and/or raspberry cullis (see p. 196). It is still best made when the three berries – raspberries, redcurrants and blackcurrants – are all available together.

*Enough thin slices of decrusted white bread to line the sides, base and top of your selected mould*

*8 oz (225 g) raspberries*

*8 oz (225 g) redcurrants, picked over*

*8 oz (225 g) blackcurrants or you can use strawberries, quartered*

## SYRUP

*⅓ pint (190 ml) water*

*8 oz (225 g) sugar*

*Juice of 1 lemon*

*2 sachets gelatine crystals*

Bring all the ingredients for the syrup to boiling point, then gradually sprinkle over the gelatine crystals, whisking them until dissolved. Crush the blackcurrants with the butt of a rolling pin and combine with the raspberries and redcurrants in a large bowl. Pour over the hot syrup and leave to cool. Line the base and sides of your chosen mould with the thin slices of bread and then, just as it is beginning to gel, ladle the fruit mixture in. Arrange a layer of bread slices on top. Put a weighted board on top to press the juices through the bread, and refrigerate overnight. Turn out on to a shallow dish to serve.

# JELLIED ORANGE FILLETS

*Serves 6–8*

✦

*I* SLIPPED this recipe into an earlier BBC publication (*Naughty but Nice*) under the Frenchified title of '*Terrine*', although it arose from my endeavours to update English recipes. It has proved so popular that I repeat it again here, together with its autumnal brother, made with blackcurrants. Both are in fact very superior fresh fruit jellies much loved by true Englishmen, and are ideal for our tables.

## JELLY SYRUP

*1 pint (570 ml) water*

*1¼ lb (550 g) caster sugar*

*Pared zest of 1 navel or Jaffa orange*

*4 sachets of gelatine crystals*

*2 tbsp Grand Marnier or Cointreau*

## FOR THE FILLING

*Zest of 3 navel or Jaffa oranges, cut into fine 'threads'*

*Up to 18 oranges*

Line a fine sieve with a piece of kitchen paper and arrange this over a 2 pint (1.1 litre) basin. Bring the sugar, orange zest and water to the boil. Remove from the heat and whisk in the gelatine crystals, sprinkling them over the hot syrup gradually. Leave to cool, but do not allow to set. Strain through the sieve to rid the syrup of any scum. Pour in the liqueur.

With a potato peeler remove the orange part only from the peel of the 3 oranges. Cut this into filaments, as fine as you can. Scald for 20 seconds in boiling water. Rinse under cold water, drain, and put into the syrup.

Knife-peel the orange pith from the 18 oranges. 'Fillet' them by cutting down either side of the membrane of each segment. (Work on a large tray or meat dish to catch any escaping juice for drinking!) Wet a mould approximately 9 × 4½ inches (23 × 11 cm) and 2½ inches (6 cm) deep, and cut a piece of greaseproof paper to just fit the base. *Pack* the mould with the orange fillets, pour over the syrup, making sure it seeps right through. Put to set.

Just before serving, run a hot palette knife gently round the sides of the mould. Invert on to a plate. Serve cut in ½ inch (1 cm) thick slices. An added luxury would be to serve the jelly with half-whipped cream, lightly sweetened, to which has been added 2 tablespoons per half-pint (275 ml) of your chosen liqueur and the finely shredded zest of 1 orange.

*Note*  This can also be made with strawberries. You will need 2 pounds (900 g) of quartered fruits to fill the mould; substitute Kirsch or Maraschino for the liqueur. Blackberries, raspberries and melon all respond well to this unusual treatment too.

# *J*ELLIED FRESH BLACKCURRANTS

*Serves 6–8*

## JELLY SYRUP

*1 pint (570 ml) water*

*1¼ lb (550 g) caster sugar*

*Finely grated zest only of 1 lemon*

*4 sachets gelatine crystals*

*Juice of ½ lemon*

*1 double gin, Kirsch or light rum*

## FOR THE FILLING

*1½ lb (700 g) fresh or defrosted blackcurrants, blueberries or bilberries*

Lightly oil with a flavourless oil a mould approximately 9 × 4½ × 2½ inches (23 × 11 × 6 cm) deep. Line with a piece of greaseproof paper, cut to fill the base. Bring the sugar, water and zest to the boil. Simmer until clear. Turn off the heat. Gradually sprinkle over the gelatine crystals, whisking them well in until completely dissolved. Strain through a fine sieve. Cool, then add your chosen liqueur and the lemon juice.

Pour a thin film of the jelly into the mould. Arrange a thin cushion of fruit on this. Pour over a little more jelly, and continue this way until the mould is packed full. Put to set. (It will *not* work by filling the mould with fruit, then pouring over the jelly in the hopes that it will seep through, as the jelly sets before this can happen. A strong jelly is required to counteract the acid juices in the fruits.)

To unmould, dip a palette knife into boiling water, and run this round the sides of the jelly. Invert on to a platter. Remove the base paper. A collar of virtually unsweetened whipped cream can be piped round the top for decoration. For this you will need ⅓ pint (190 ml) of double cream to which you can add 1 teaspoon of caster or icing sugar and 1 tablespoon of your chosen liqueur.

# *P*EARS IN SWEET WHITE WINE WITH CANDIED LEMON SPIRALS

*Serves 2*

*2 large ripe comice pears*

*2 lemons, juice and rind (see method)*

*2 oz (50 g) caster sugar*

*½ pint (275 ml) sweet white wine*

To prepare the fruit prettily and effectively, you will need a cannelle knife. These are readily available from good cookshops. With the knife, starting at the top of one of the lemons, carefully cut round and round in one long cut, finishing with a striped-looking lemon and a long string of lemon peel. Repeat this with the second lemon. Now squeeze the juice of the lemons into a basin.

Using a potato peeler, cut out the 'flower' end of each pear, removing about an inch of the core from up and inside the pear. Then peel the fruit, leaving the stalk intact if possible (this is purely for effect). With the cannelle knife, cut a spiral wedge out of the pear flesh, starting at the base of the fruit and spiralling up to the top. Leave ¾ inch (1.5 cm) between each spiral at the base end. Bathe the pears in lemon juice.

In a small enamel or stainless steel pan just large enough to contain the two pears on their sides, nose to tail, bring the remaining lemon juice to the boil, with the sugar, wine and strips of lemon rind. Simmer the pears in this until they appear translucent and are cooked. You should turn them, using two tablespoons, every 5 minutes or so. When cooked, remove the pears to a small serving dish and chill.

Continue boiling the wine syrup until it is *almost* as thick as warm golden syrup. Leave to cool, then chill. Remove the strips of lemon peel and cut into suitable lengths to press into the 'gullies' in each pear. Spoon a little of the syrup over each pear and serve.

Any remaining syrup can be stored in an airtight container in the refrigerator for later use with fruit salad, pancakes, waffles, or to make apple purée, etc. It keeps for months.

# *F*RESH PINEAPPLE, MELON AND PEAR SALAD

*Serves 6–8*

*T*HE secret of this – if secret there be – is in the cutting of the fruit: the pieces must be small and of equal size.

*1 small pineapple*

*2 comice pears*

*1 ogen melon or ¹/2 a honeydew melon*

*Juice of 1 lemon*

*2 oz (50 g) caster sugar*

*1 tbsp water*

*1 tbsp Kirsch, Pear William, Cointreau or gin*

Bring the sugar and water to the boil, and simmer until clear. Cool. Stir in the Kirsch or other liqueur.

Using a sharp serrated knife, peel and core the pineapple by cutting off the top and base; then, from the top, push the point of the knife right down to the base within ¼ inch (0.5 cm) of the skin. The knife must be held vertically. Using an 'upright' sawing motion cut right round the fruit. Push the cylinder of pineapple out. Cut this in half lengthways, then in half again. Cut away the core. Cut each quarter in half again, then into small pieces.

To prepare the melon, cut a shaving off the top and bottom. Using a sharp knife, cut round and down to remove the skin. Cut the peeled melon in half. With a spoon, scoop out and discard the seeds. Proceed to cut the flesh as for the pineapple.

Peel, core and cut the pears into pieces the same size, tossing them in the lemon juice to retain their white colour. Mix all the fruits together in the cooled syrup. Cover with plastic film. Chill for 4 hours.

# Lemon and Grape Jelly

*Serves 6*

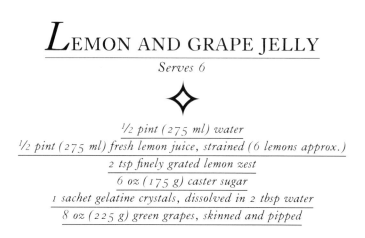

*½ pint (275 ml) water*

*½ pint (275 ml) fresh lemon juice, strained (6 lemons approx.)*

*2 tsp finely grated lemon zest*

*6 oz (175 g) caster sugar*

*1 sachet gelatine crystals, dissolved in 2 tbsp water*

*8 oz (225 g) green grapes, skinned and pipped*

Divide the grapes among 6 wine glasses. Bring the water, lemon juice, zest and sugar to boiling point. Stir in the melted gelatine. Leave to cool, then strain. Ladle into the glasses and put to set.

# Stock Syrup for
# Water Ices

*1¼ lb (550 g) caster sugar*

*1½ pints (900 ml) water*

*3½ fl oz (85 ml) glucose syrup*

(Glucose syrup is available from dispensing chemists and high-class grocers.)

Bring all the ingredients together in a meticulously clean pan. Bubble for 2–3 minutes, when the syrup will be quite clear. Cool, then strain through a conical sieve to rid the syrup of any possible scum thrown off by the sugar or water. Store in a screw-topped jar in the refrigerator. The syrup will keep for some weeks.

# *L*EMON ICE

*Serves 6–8*

*½ pint (275 ml) fresh lemon juice, strained (about 6 lemons)*

*½ egg white, beaten slightly*

*1 pint (570 ml) stock syrup*

Bring all the ingredients together and churn, following the instructions on your particular machine. Use the lemon skins to make a lemon drink. Grated zest is undesirable in this very refined ice.

# *C*OCONUT ICE-CREAM WITH PLUM SAUCE

*Serves 6*

*1 pint (570 ml) single cream*

*6 oz (175 g) freshly grated or desiccated coconut*

*4 oz (110 g) caster sugar*

*8 egg yolks*

*2 fl oz (50 ml) cream of coconut (coconut milk)*

*¼ pint (150 ml) double cream whipped to soft peak*

## *P*LUM SAUCE

*8 Gaviota plums or red plums (about 1¼ lb: 550 g), quartered*

*3 oz (75 g) caster sugar*

*2 tbsp water*

*1 tbsp Kirsch (optional)*

In a non-stick pan bring the coconut and single cream to the boil. Turn off the heat, leave to infuse, and cool for an hour. Strain through a sieve, then put the coconut into a clean linen cloth, gather the fabric round it in a roll and squeeze, twisting each end in opposing directions. Discard the coconut except for 1 tablespoonful.

In a bowl, whisk the sugar, cream of coconut and egg yolks until light and fluffy. Whisk in the pint (570 ml) of coconut-flavoured cream. Pour the mixture back into the non-stick pan, bring to the boil very slowly, stirring all the time with a straight-edged spatula, until the mixture thickens. As for a custard do not allow to boil. Cool in a sink of cold water. Whisk in the half-whipped cream and churn.

Bring the sugar and water for the sauce to the boil. Add the quartered plums and simmer, covered, until soft. Cool, then press through a fine sieve. Stir in the Kirsch; chill, well covered with plastic film.

# Orange Water Ice

*Serves 6–8*

*1 pint (570 ml) fresh orange juice, from blood oranges*

*½ egg white, beaten slightly*

*1 pint (570 ml) stock syrup*

*2 fl oz (50 ml) Grand Marnier*

Proceed as for the Lemon Ice, adding the liqueur just as the ice is beginning to ribbon in the churn.

On a hot summer day substitute 1 fluid ounce (25 ml) of triple-strength orange flower water for the stronger liqueur: a perfect effect is created if the ice is served with sliced strawberries, splashed with orange-flower water and dredged lightly with icing sugar.

# Summer Fruit Salad Ice

*Serves 8–10*

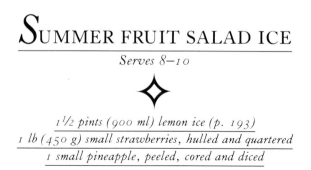

*1½ pints (900 ml) lemon ice (p. 193)*

*1 lb (450 g) small strawberries, hulled and quartered*

*1 small pineapple, peeled, cored and diced*

Add the fruit to the lemon ice when it reaches the soft ribbon stage when churning. Any left-over fruit can be served as an added garnish.

# $A$PPLE AND ROSE PETAL CREAM ICE

*Serves 12*

*I* WANTED this ice-cream to be evocative of an English garden. I think I've achieved my aim: it would be perfect for a summer wedding.

*³/4 pint (400 ml) stock syrup*
*³/4 pint (400 ml) concentrated apple juice*
*¹/2 egg white, beaten lightly*
*3 tsp rose-flower water*
*3 drops only red colouring*
*¹/3 pint (190 ml) double cream, whipped to soft peak*

Put all the ingredients, except the cream, into your churn. When the ice is ribboning and looks a delicate creamy pink, spoon in the cream. Serve small amounts in a wine glass, with a crystallised rose petal or two. This ice-cream keeps, but crystals will form if it is kept too cold.

# $R$HUBARB ICE

*Serves 4–6*

*M*OST of us remember rhubarb as something acid: pinkish-grey knitting wool adrift in a sea of sour juice. In this recipe the full tart flavour of the fruit glows with national pride!

*2 lb (900 g) rhubarb, trimmed and cut into 1 inch (2.5 cm) pieces*
*1 fl oz (25 ml) gin*
*¹/2 oz (10 g) unsalted butter*
*4 oz (110 g) caster sugar*
*1 tbsp cold water*

## SYRUP

*6 oz (175 g) caster sugar*
*2 tbsp cold water*

Put the rhubarb, sugar, butter, gin and water into a pan. Cover and toss over a low heat until the juices start to draw. Simmer until fallen to a mush. Blend and rub through a fine sieve. Do not cool yet.

Bring the second amount of sugar to the boil and boil to 'hard ball', (248°F 120°C). If you don't possess a sugar thermometer, boil rapidly until the sugar is making a 'rich' bubbling noise, is thick, and *just about* to turn colour: you will notice this stage if you watch the edges of the syrup as it boils. Do not stir. Pour this syrup into the rhubarb purée. Now cool, and churn in the ice-cream maker for 20 minutes to a soft, spoonable texture. It will look pale-pink and creamy. Store in the freezer.

# *R*ASPBERRY CULLIS

*Serves 6–8*

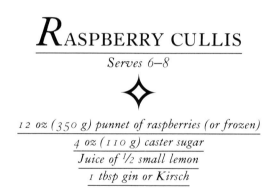

*12 oz (350 g) punnet of raspberries (or frozen)*
*4 oz (110 g) caster sugar*
*Juice of ½ small lemon*
*1 tbsp gin or Kirsch*

Purée all of the ingredients in a blender, then rub through a fine sieve to remove the seeds. Chill well, covered with plastic film.

# *B*LACKCURRANT PURÉE

*Makes about 1¾ pints (1 litre)*

*F*OR ice-cream, jelly or sauce, or just for freezing and storing.

*1½ lb (700 g) blackcurrants, fresh or frozen*
*8 oz (225 g) caster sugar*
*⅛ pint (75 ml) water*

Pick over the blackcurrants carefully, then bring all the ingredients slowly to the boil together in a pan. Cool, then strain and rub the purée through a fine sieve.

# *B*ROWN BREAD ICE-CREAM WITH RUM

*Serves 6–8*

*T*HIS ice-cream was a great favourite with the Victorians and Edwardians, and it made a regular appearance during the summer months in my home, but always made with soft crumbs. I use crisp crumbs, as you will see. Different, not just better!

## *B*ASIC CUSTARD ICE-CREAM

*1 pint (570 ml) single cream*
*½ vanilla pod or 1 tsp vanilla essence*
*8 egg yolks*
*3 oz (75 g) caster sugar*
*3 tbsp Jamaica rum*

## *B*ROWN BREAD

*6 oz (175 g) good rich brown breadcrumbs*
*2 oz (50 g) unsalted butter, melted*
*2 oz (50 g) caster sugar*

Beat the egg yolks and sugar until creamy white and fluffy in a non-stick pan. Bring the cream to boiling point with the vanilla pod (or essence). Remove the pod, and pour the cream over the egg mixture, whisking briskly. Return the mixture to the pan, and over the lowest possible heat stir all the time, covering the base of the pan meticulously, until the custard coats the back of a wooden spoon well. Pour into a bowl and leave to cool. Add the rum to the cooled custard. Churn, following the instructions on your particular machine.

Gently fry the breadcrumbs in the butter, patiently stirring them around in the pan. Sprinkle over the sugar and let this caramelise. Cool. Crush to fine crumbs with a rolling pin. Put half this mixture into the ice-cream just as it is beginning to set. Serve the remainder as a crunchy topping with a spoonful or two of thick cream as well.

# HOT PUDDINGS

◇

*Traditionally, Englishwomen have excelled at the arts of cake, biscuit and bread-making, as well as preparing jams, preserves and pickles. The creation of melting-in-the-mouth pastry for pies and tarts, of the lightest of sponge puddings, or the richest of fruit cakes – these are still their strengths. Perhaps, though, I might be allowed to suggest gently that some of these old favourites can be given an even lighter touch by adapting the methods I describe here. Given these wings of flight, a reliable old warhorse such as Bread and Butter Pudding will become a soaring Pegasus! Make the most of the tartness of fresh fruit in delicious accompanying sauces; or indulge yourself just once in a while with a touch of cream.*

# BREAD AND BUTTER PUDDING

*Serves 6–8*

$M$Y first efforts to update this national pudding appeared in the *Yorkshire Post* almost 15 years ago, when I used a milk custard, but still included quite a lot of bread *cubes* and certainly too much jam. More recently, in *Just Desserts* for BBC Pebble Mill, I lightened it still further. Here, I have gone as far as I think it possible without losing sight of its name. Bread is at a minimum, the light rich custard is made with cream, the fruit is liquor-soaked and the modest amount of jam is sieved. The result? . . . *ambrosia!*

*6 oz (175 g) seedless raisins or sultanas,
soaked overnight in 2–3 tbsp sherry, whisky, brandy or gin!*

*8 thin slices of good white bread, without crusts*

*2 oz (50 g) softened unsalted butter*

*4 oz (110 g) sieved apricot jam*

*10 fl oz (275 ml) double cream*

*10 fl oz (275 ml) rich milk*

*3 large eggs, beaten with 2 extra egg yolks*

*2 oz (50 g) caster sugar*

*½ vanilla pod or 1 tsp of vanilla essence*

*A dredging of icing sugar*

Choose a large 10 inch (25.5 cm) diameter round or oval dish, 1½–2 inches (3.5–5 cm) deep. Butter this with a little unsalted butter. Scatter the soaked raisins over the bottom.

Butter the bread and make four large jam sandwiches (these can be made the day before and stored in a sandwich bag). Cut into 6 pieces, or cut into circles using a cutter small enough to give you approximately 5 rings. Arrange these, overlapping if necessary, around the perimeter of the dish.

Preheat the oven to gas mark 3, 325°F (170°C). Beat the eggs with the sugar. Bring the milk, vanilla and cream to the boil (*slowly* if you are using a pod, so that the essence is extracted from it). Pour the hot liquid over the egg mixture and mix thoroughly, using a balloon whisk. Now, *ladle* the custard over the bread pieces, so they get well soaked, but are not disarranged. Place the dish in a water bath large enough to contain it without overflowing, and bake for 45 minutes to 1 hour, or until the custard is just set and the bread lightly browned. Dredge with icing sugar. Wipe the edge of the dish.

Serve hot or cold, or for added effect — and flavour — you can caramelise the top under a preheated, spanking hot grill, then leave to cool and serve cold. Serve with double pouring cream or fresh apricot purée — though this really would be gilding the lily.

A variation can be made with brown bread, brown sugar and rum, as I believe John Tovey does to great effect at Miller Howe.

# *Q*UEEN'S PUDDINGS

### Serves 6–8

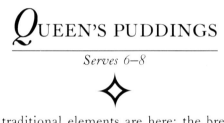

*A*GAIN all the traditional elements are here: the bread, however, now plays a subservient role!

| |
|---|
| *½ pint (275 ml) single cream* |
| *½ pint (275 ml) rich milk* |
| *1 tsp finely grated lemon rind* |
| *2 oz (50 g) caster sugar* |
| *4 small eggs, beaten* |
| *1 oz (25 g) or 1 tbsp fresh white breadcrumbs, finely grated* |

## *M*ERINGUE TOPPING

| |
|---|
| *2 large egg whites* |
| *2 oz (50 g) caster sugar* |

## *T*O GARNISH

| |
|---|
| *Lemon curd, or redcurrant jelly, or sieved raspberry jam* |

Preheat the oven to gas mark 3, 325°F (170°C). Lightly butter 6–8 ramekins. In a non-stick pan bring the milk, cream, lemon rind and sugar to the boil. Pour over the beaten eggs, whisking well. Stir in the modest amount of breadcrumbs. Ladle the mixture into the ramekins and stand them in a water bath to bake until they are set.

For the meringue topping, whisk the egg whites until stiff and then whisk in the caster sugar. Using a piping-bag fitted with a plain ⅛ inch (0.25 cm) tube, pipe a collar of this topping round the rim of each ramekin and make a criss-cross pattern across the surface of each. Add a blob of lemon curd, jam or jelly. Return to the oven for a further 5–10 minutes for the meringue to set and brown, or stand the puddings under a medium-hot grill.

The puddings can be served cold, but in this case the 'custard' will be firmer, so use only 3 eggs. You can, of course, make one single big pudding. Pipe the meringue in 1 inch (2.5 cm) squares to create a lattice pattern and make a mosaic of colour by decorating with different jams at will.

# *B*AKED APRICOT RUM PUDDINGS

*Serves 8*

8 apricot caps, fresh, tinned or dried

2 tbsp apricot jam, sieved

4 oz (110 g) unsalted butter, softened

4 oz (110 g) caster sugar

2 large eggs, beaten

1 tsp vanilla essence

4 oz (110 g) S.R. flour

1 level tsp baking powder

1 oz (25 g) cornflour, sieved twice with the flour and baking powder

2 tbsp or more demerara rum

Preheat the oven to gas mark 5, 375°F (190°C). Butter 8 individual deep bun tins well and place a teaspoonful of sieved jam and an apricot half in the bottom of each.

Cream the butter and sugar until light and fluffy, beat in the eggs and vanilla essence, adding a dredge of flour as you do so if the mixture shows signs of curdling (because it's too cold). Cut and fold the flours well in. Mix to a soft dropping consistency with the rum (or milk, or water). Spoon into the tins to two-thirds full. Bake in the preheated oven for 20–25 minutes, or until risen and firm to the touch. Turn out on to warm pudding plates and serve with English custard or thick cream.

# REDCURRANT AND HAZELNUT ROLY-POLY PUDDING

*Serves 6–8*

✧

*T*HIS pudding, with its two sauces, can be served either hot or cold.

## NUT SPONGE MIXTURE

*2 large eggs*

*2 oz (50 g) caster sugar*

*3 oz (75 g) finely-crushed, well-toasted hazelnuts, mixed with 1 oz (25 g) S.R. flour*

## FILLING

*8 oz (225 g) redcurrant jelly*

*3 oz (75 g) roughly crushed, well-toasted hazelnuts*

## REDCURRANT SAUCE

*1 lb (450 g) fresh or frozen redcurrants*

*2 oz (50 g) caster sugar*

## HONEY-CREAM SAUCE

*1/2 pint (275 ml) double cream*

*1 tbsp Hymettus honey*

*2 tsp lemon juice*

First of all, prepare the redcurrant sauce. Pick over the redcurrants, discarding any spoiled ones, and then, in a non-stick pan over minimal heat, bring them to the boil with the sugar. Simmer until the fruit collapses (2 minutes). Cool, and purée by rubbing through a fine-meshed sieve. Chill. Stir the ingredients for the honey-cream sauce together, and chill as well.

Preheat the oven to gas mark 7, 425°F (220°C). Butter a swiss roll tin approximately 14 × 8 inches (35.5 × 20.5 cm), and line it with buttered paper.

Cream the eggs and sugar until they are fluffy and the whisk leaves a trail. Cut and fold in the nuts and flour. Pour the mixture into the lined tin and bake for 12 minutes only, near the top of the oven.

Have ready a tea towel wrung out in cold water and arranged horizontally on a flat surface. On top of this place a sheet of greaseproof paper slightly larger than the tin. Dredge it well and *evenly* with caster sugar (about 1 tablespoonful). Turn the baked sponge immediately onto this, and spread evenly with the filling which you have prepared by warming the jelly in a basin over a pan of boiling water, and then mixing in the nuts. Carefully, but firmly, roll the sponge up, starting with the edge nearest to you, and rolling towards the back. Use the cloth and paper to help you, but make sure you trap neither in the roll.

Serve immediately with both the sauces, or leave to cool, in which case dredge the roll with icing sugar and cut on the diagonal into 6–8 pieces.

# *B*AKED WALNUT ORANGE PUDDINGS

*Serves 8: can be eaten hot or cold*

4 oz (110 g) unsalted butter, softened

3 oz (75 g) caster sugar

2 large eggs, beaten

1 tbsp Golden Syrup

1 tsp finely grated orange rind

1 tsp vanilla essence

3 oz (75 g) S.R. flour

1 tsp baking powder

3 oz (75 g) finely crushed walnuts

1/8 pint (75 ml) orange juice, for mixing

2 tsp finely grated orange rind

## *H*ONEY-WALNUT SAUCE

1/4 pint (150 ml) double cream

1 tbsp orange blossom honey

1 tbsp orange flower water

2 tbsp fully crushed walnuts

## *To* GARNISH

*8 walnut halves*

*Chopped candied orange or mixed peel*

Preheat the oven to gas mark 5, 375°F (190°C). Butter 8 individual bun tins and line with buttered papers.

Cream the butter, sugar, syrup, vanilla essence and orange rind. Beat in the eggs. Mix the flour, baking powder and walnuts together, then cut and fold into the mixture. Mix to a soft dropping consistency with the orange juice. Fill each tin up to two-thirds full with the mixture and bake in the preheated oven for 25–30 minutes. Leave to cool for 10 minutes, whether being served hot or cold. Run a pointed knife round the sides of each tin and turn out.

Make the sauce by stirring the cream, honey and orange flower water together over a low heat until just under boiling point. Mix in the crushed walnuts. Garnish each pudding with a walnut half and a little chopped peel. Pour the sauce over, if serving hot.

# *P*LUM PUDDINGS

*Serves 8*

*W*HO would have thought that almost the same ingredients that we use in what is perhaps our oldest — and virtually our national — pudding could become the confection I give you here!

*16 ripe plums: 8 split and pitted, 8 left whole for baking*

*Up to 4 oz (110 g) almond paste or commercial marzipan*

## *P*ASTRY

*8 oz (225 g) soft white cake flour*

*2 oz (50 g) icing sugar*

*3 oz (75 g) unsalted butter, cubed and chilled*

*3 oz (75 g) pure refined lard, cubed and chilled*

*1 large whole egg, beaten*

*Sugar syrup (optional)*

## FOR THE SUGAR GLAZE

*2 tbsp caster sugar*

*1 tbsp water*

## CREAM SAUCE

*½ pint (275 ml) single cream*

*4 egg yolks*

*1 oz (25 g) caster sugar*

*2 tbsp Kirsch or gin*

Preheat the oven to gas mark 7, 425°F (220°C). Make the pastry in a food processor, or in the usual way. It is a soft mixture, tricky to handle, but worth the hassle.

Divide the almond paste into 8 pieces. Roll and shape each one between your hands to the size and shape of a plumstone. Press the two halves of the split plums round these.

Roll the pastry out separately to enwrap each plum – you'll need approximately an 8 inch (20.5 cm) circle. Envelop the plum in this. Stand each one on a lightly buttered baking tray. Bake in the preheated oven for 25–30 minutes, or until crisp and golden-brown. Brush with sugar glaze, prepared by boiling the sugar with the water until it reaches the 'hard ball' stage. Serve hot, warm or cold, with the cream sauce. Make this by creaming the egg yolks and sugar together until light and fluffy. Bring the cream to the boil in a non-stick pan, and pour over the egg mixture, whisking briskly. Return the pan to minimal heat, stirring all the time until the sauce has thickened. Remove from the heat, strain into a pyrex bowl, and add the liqueur. If served warm, keep over a pan of hot, not boiling, water. Otherwise, cool, then chill, covered with plastic film.

Bake the remaining 8 plums, without water, separately until just soft. Serve a baked plum with a pastry plum on a pool of sauce.

*Page 207 Rich Rice Pudding*
*Page 208 Chilled Semolina Pudding*

# STEAMED CARAMEL PUDDING

*Serves 6*

*3 eggs*

*3 oz (75 g) caster sugar*

*1 tsp grated lemon zest*

*3 oz (75 g) S.R. flour, sieved*

## CARAMEL SAUCE

*⅛ pint (75 ml) caramel (see below)*

*¼ pint (150 ml) double cream*

Butter a 2 pint (1.1 litre) pudding basin, and a piece of foil, pleated, ready to use for a cover. Have the steamer boiling. Put 2 tablespoons of caramel, prepared as described below, in the bottom of the basin.

Whisk the eggs with the sugar and lemon zest until the whisk leaves a distinct trail. Cut and thoroughly fold in the flour. Pour into the pudding basin, cover and steam for 1½ hours.

Over a low heat warm the caramel for the sauce until runny: stir in the cream and bring almost to boiling point. Do not boil. Turn the pudding out on to a serving dish. Pour the sauce over.

*Note*   This pudding becomes steamed jam sponge when 2 tablespoons of sieved raspberry or apricot jam are substituted for the caramel, in which case serve with a raspberry or apricot sauce.

## TO MAKE CARAMEL

*4 oz (110 g) caster sugar*

*4 tbsp water*

Bring the sugar and water to boiling point, stirring from time to time to ensure the crystals are dissolved. (Use an aluminium, stainless steel or copper pan for this. The high heat may crack enamel.) Boil rapidly until you have a good, deep caramel colour. Use a cloth to protect the hand and stand the pan *in* the sink. Fill a soup ladle with 3 fluid ounces (75 ml) of cold water. Pour this into the caramel. It will splutter and steam. Return the pan to the heat and simmer for a few seconds until the caramel is evenly melted. Cool before use.

Any spare caramel can be stored indefinitely. It may set a little and will need to be softened by standing the container in a pan of hot water before reusing.

# *B*AKED ALMOND
## SPONGE PUDDING
## WITH COFFEE CREAM SAUCE

*Serves 6–8*

*T*HIS recipe doubles, when served cold, as a light cake, but does not keep well.

*4 whole eggs*

*4 oz (110 g) caster sugar*

*4 oz (110 g) S.R. flour, sieved with 1 level tsp baking powder*

*2 oz (50 g) toasted ground almonds*

### *C*OFFEE CREAM SAUCE

*2 tbsp coffee essence, made with 2 heaped tbsp medium to high roast coffee (see method)*

*1½ oz (40 g) muscovado sugar*

*1 tbsp brandy*

*¼ pint (150 ml) double cream*

Preheat the oven to gas mark 4, 350°F (180°C). Butter a deep, non-stick cake tin, 7 inch (18 cm) diameter, and line with buttered paper. Whisk the eggs and sugar until light and fluffy and the whisk leaves a distinct trail in the mixture. Mix the almonds with the flour. Using a balloon whisk, cut and thoroughly fold in the almond and flour mixture. Pour into the prepared cake tin.

Bake on the centre shelf of the preheated oven for 30 minutes, or until the mixture is just springy to the touch. Serve hot with cold coffee cream sauce. You need to prepare this in advance to allow it to become well chilled;

first make the coffee essence. Pour ½ pint (275 ml) boiling water over the coffee and stir well. Leave to cool. Decant first through a fine-meshed sieve, then again through the sieve lined with a piece of kitchen paper towel. Cool, then chill. Any spare can be used for drinking. Dissolve the sugar in the coffee essence and brandy over a low heat. Remove from the heat and allow to cool. Stir in the cream: then, using a hand whisk, whip the cream until it is as thick as pouring cream. Cover with plastic film and chill until ready to serve (it will thicken even more during this time).

# *A*PPLE AND LEMON TARTS WITH BILBERRY SAUCE WITH GIN

*Serves 8*

*T*HE distinctive flavour of bilberries gathered from the moors in the north of England is not to be missed. However, these tiny, dark blue-black berries are not always available, so substitute blackcurrants or blackberries. The sauce is also an excellent accompaniment to vanilla ice-cream.

*³/4 lb (350 g) rich shortcrust pastry (see p. 217)*

### *F*OR THE FILLING

*1 lb (450 g) Cox's apples, peeled, cored and sliced*

*2 oz (50 g) unsalted butter*

*1 level tbsp finely grated lemon zest*

*1 tbsp lemon juice*

*2 oz caster sugar*

### *B*ILBERRY SAUCE WITH GIN

*8 oz (225 g) bilberries*

*3 oz (75 g) caster sugar*

*1 tbsp lemon juice*

*1 tbsp gin*

Roll out and cut the pastry to fit 8 × 2½ inch (6 cm) tartlet tins. Bake blind at gas mark 7, 425°F (220°C) for 5–6 minutes. Lower the temperature to gas mark 4, 350°F (180°C) for a further 7–8 minutes, or until the pastry is golden-brown and crisp right through. Carefully take the tarts out of the tins and cool on a cooling tray.

In a pan, melt the butter without colouring it, add the apples and lemon juice, put a lid on the pan, and toss over a medium to low heat until the apples start to soften. Add the sugar and cook to a pulp. Blend to a fine purée. Add the lemon zest after blending. Cool.

To make the sauce, put the bilberries and lemon juice into a pan over a low heat until the juices start to draw. Stir in the sugar and cook for a minute or two more until the fruit is totally soft. Cool, then press through a fine-meshed sieve. Stir in the gin and chill, covered with plastic film. Fill the pastry shells just before serving, and serve the sauce separately.

# *P*EAR TARTS

*Serves 8*

*1 lb (450 g) rich shortcrust pastry (see p. 217)*
*1½ lb (700 g) comice pears, to yield 1 lb (450 g) purée*
*2 oz (50 g) unsalted butter*
*2 oz (50 g) caster sugar*
*2 tsp grated lemon zest*
*1 heaped tsp arrowroot slaked in the lemon juice*
*Juice of 1 lemon*

Make 8 pastry shells, as in the previous recipe. Prepare the filling. Melt the butter, add the pears and sugar, and toss over a low heat. Cover, and simmer until tender. Blend to a fine purée. It will be a little liquid, so bring it to the boil in a pan, stir in the slaked arrowroot, and bubble until thick. Stir in the grated lemon zest. Cool, and cover with plastic film until ready for use. Fill the pastry shells with the purée just before serving.

*Note* 1 level teaspoonful of ground cinnamon can be used as a change from lemon juice, in which case slake the arrowroot with 2 tablespoons of water.

# *P*ANCAKES

*Serves 8*

*I* THOUGHT the pancakes I devised in my book *Fine English Cookery* back in 1972 were good – these are exquisite! Serve them with lemon and icing sugar (caster sugar is too gritty for these velvety pancakes).

*4 oz (110 g) plain white flour sieved with 1 tbsp caster sugar and ¼ tsp salt*

*4 large eggs, beaten*

*½ pint (275 ml) milk, enriched with ¼ pint (150 ml) single cream*

*Clarified butter for frying*

*Icing sugar for dredging*

Put the sieved flour into a bowl. Make a well and pour in the beaten eggs. Mix to a smooth paste using a balloon whisk. Gradually incorporate the enriched milk. Strain through a sieve into a clean bowl. Leave to mature for at least 2 hours.

Using a well-heated 6 inch (15 cm) pancake pan, pour in a scant teaspoon of the butter and swirl round (or brush the pan with butter). Pour in 1 fluid ounce (25 ml) of the batter. Swirl round to the edges of the pan and fry until the batter has set, lifting the pan away from the heat if the edges appear to be catching, rather than lowering the heat. When set, turn over and cook for a few seconds only on the second side. Turn on to a clean work surface and fold or roll. Keep warm on a dinner plate over a pan of simmering water covered with a clean towel. Dredge with icing sugar. This quantity should yield 20–24 pancakes.

# *W*HISKY BUTTERCREAM PANCAKES

*Serves 6*

*18 small pancakes*

## WHISKY BUTTERCREAM

*3 oz (75 g) unsalted butter, softened*
*2 oz (50 g) icing sugar, sieved*
*2 tsp lemon juice*
*1 fl oz (25 ml) whisky*

Beat the butter and icing sugar until light and fluffy. Beat in the juice and whisky. Spread ½ ounce (10 g) of the buttercream on to each pancake. Roll them up or fold them, and place in a shallow ovenproof dish to warm through in the oven, covered with foil, at gas mark 6, 400°F (200°C) for 5–6 minutes. Remove, and dredge with extra icing sugar.

For added luxury, have ready 2 fluid ounces (50 ml) of whisky, warmed in a teacup that is standing in a pan of boiling water (this way the alcohol cannot ignite unexpectedly!). Pour it over the pancakes at the table, ignite, and let the flames die down. Serve with walnut ice-cream if liked.

*Note* An excellent variation on this theme is to substitute muscovado sugar for icing sugar, and light or dark rum for whisky.

# *B*URN'T CREAM PANCAKES

*Serves 6*

*18 pancakes*

## *F*OR THE SAUCE

*4 egg yolks*
*½ pint (275 ml) double cream, boiling*
*1 tsp vanilla essence*
*Icing sugar (see method)*

Allow the pancakes to cool. Fold each one into four and arrange, slightly overlapping, in a shallow, round fireproof dish, approximately 9 inches (23 cm) in diameter. Preheat the oven to gas mark 6, 400°F (200°C). Mix the egg yolks, cream and vanilla essence together in a small bowl. Spoon over the pancakes, ensuring that the 'open' edge is coated.

Set the grill to high. Heat the pancakes through in the preheated oven until the cream just starts to set. Dredge with a good coating of icing sugar, wipe the edges of the dish, put to caramelise under the grill.

*Note*   For extra luxury the pancakes can first be spread with sieved apricot jam or pear purée (see p. 212 – make up half this quantity).

# *M*INI SPONGE PUDDINGS

*Makes 10–12*

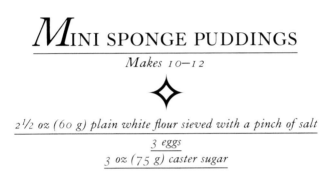

2½ oz (60 g) plain white flour sieved with a pinch of salt

3 eggs

3 oz (75 g) caster sugar

Preheat the oven to gas mark 4, 350°F (180°C). Lightly but thoroughly brush 10–12 bun tins or fancy moulds with melted butter. Dredge each tin with caster sugar, shaking away any spare (this will reveal the bald patches!).

Mix the sugar and whole eggs in a pyrex basin which will sit comfortably inside the top of a pan of simmering water. Using a rotary whisk, whisk the mixture gently but thoroughly until it is pale, thick, and forms a ribbon when the whisk is drawn through it. Remove the basin from the heat, and continue whisking gently until the mixture cools a little. Now, using a balloon whisk, cut and fold the flour into the egg mixture. Spoon the mixture into the prepared tins, filling them approximately two-thirds full. Rap each tin sharply on the worktop to settle. Sprinkle a good pinch or two of caster sugar on top. Bake for 12–15 minutes, when the puddings should be firm to the touch. Serve warm or cold with any sweet sauce you like.

# *F*LAKY PASTRY

*T*HE smallest viable amount when making flaky pastry is 1 lb (450 g) of flour and 1 lb (450 g) of butter. Flaky pastry can be stored almost indefinitely in the freezer in ½ lb (225 g) pieces.

$$1 \; lb \; (450 \; g) \; plain \; white \; flour$$
$$\frac{1}{2} \; tsp \; salt$$
$$1 \; lb \; (450 \; g) \; unsalted \; butter$$
$$7 \; fl \; oz \; (200 \; ml) \; cold \; water$$
$$1 \; tsp \; lemon \; juice$$

Sieve the flour and salt into a bowl. With your fingers or a pastry cutter cut or rub in 4 oz (110 g) of the butter. Stir in the water and lemon juice with a fork. Turn the dough onto a floured board and knead it until it is pliable. Form into an oblong shape, put into a floured plastic bag, and leave to rest in the refrigerator for 2 hours. (This will make the gluten in the flour more elastic, making the pastry more workable.)

Place the remaining butter between two sheets of plastic film and, with a rolling pin, work it into a rectangle roughly 7 × 4 inches (18 × 10 cm). The butter should be workable but not too soft; if it is too soft put it back in the fridge. Now roll the rested dough into a rectangle 14 × 8 inches (35.5 × 20.5 cm). Keep the work surface lightly dredged with flour, but use a pastry brush to remove any excess flour from the pastry as you roll. Set the block of butter centrally on the rolled dough. Roll out the sides where the butter is, by an inch (2.5 cm) or so, and then fold these two flaps over the ends of the butter block. Now fold the top of the dough over to the bottom edge of the butter. Brush away any flour. Bring the bottom dough up and over to the top edge, forming a neat parcel.

Turn the pastry clockwise so that the flaps are like a book. Gently press the open side, top edge and bottom edge with the rolling pin. Then starting at the top, press very gently at ½ inch (1 cm) intervals down the block of pastry, using light even pressure with both hands and watching carefully that you don't press it out of line or push the butter through. Gradually start *rolling* the pastry until you have a rectangle the same size as the one you started with. Brush the surface of the pastry again, dredging the work surface if necessary. Fold the pastry exactly as before and roll again, folding in exactly the same way. You have now given the pastry a double turn. Slide the block of pastry into a plastic bag and put to set in the refrigerator for 1 hour. This will harden up the butter again.

Repeat the process again – rolling, folding, turning twice – *gently* pressing at ½ inch (1 cm) intervals before gradually changing to a light rolling movement over the whole surface of the pastry. Take care at all times that the butter never bursts through the pastry. (If there are any signs of this happening return the pastry to the refrigerator to set the butter.) Return the pastry, in a plastic bag, to the refrigerator for 1 hour more. When you are ready to use it, roll and fold twice as before. You now have hundreds (486 to be exact) of layers of pastry and butter which, when baked in a hot oven, gas mark 7, 425°F (220°C), will puff up into delicate, butter-crisp layers. If you remember that you are aiming to have the butter and 'dough' at the same consistency so that you are not forcing one against the other, you won't go wrong.

# *R*ICH SHORTCRUST PASTRY

*9 oz (250 g) plain white flour*

*5 oz (150 g) unsalted butter, cut into small cubes*

*1 oz (25 g) lard, cut into cubes*

*1 egg, beaten*

*1 level tsp salt*

Sieve the flour with the salt into a basin. Make a well and put in this the butter, lard and beaten egg. 'Peck' and pinch the mixture together, gradually incorporating the flour from the sides of the well as you go along, so that it eventually forms into a dough. Knead lightly, and make into whatever shape you want, e.g. square, round, oval. Slide the shape into a floured plastic bag and refrigerate for 1 hour or more.

# *C*HOUX PASTRY

### *Makes 20–30 buns*

*T*HIS pastry has endless uses, both sweet and savoury. The choux buns can be made in advance and either frozen or stored in an airtight container.

*7½ fl oz (210 ml) water and milk, mixed*

*2½ oz (60 g) unsalted butter, cubed*

*3¾ oz (90 g) plain white flour sieved with ¼ tsp salt and ½ tsp caster sugar*

*3 large eggs, lightly beaten*

## TO GLAZE

*1 small egg beaten with 1 tbsp milk*

Preheat the oven to gas mark 6, 400°F (200°C). Bring the butter, water and milk to the boil in a pan; remove from the heat. Have the flour, salt and sugar sieved onto a paper. Tip this at one fell swoop into the pan, stir in, and beat vigorously with a wooden spatula.

Return the pan to a low heat; mix in and gently beat the mixture until it has dried a little and has formed a single ball of paste. Tip this into a bowl. Gradually beat in the beaten eggs: this can be arduous as you have to continue beating until the mixture acquires a silky sheen. The operation can be done in a food processor: if you do this, be careful not to overwork the paste.

Brush a baking sheet with a little melted butter — heavy-handed buttering of the sheet creates crusty bases to the buns. Pipe or spoon the required shapes onto this. Brush each shape very lightly with beaten egg and milk (this is optional). Bake in the preheated oven for 10, 15 or 20 minutes, depending on their size. Frankly, I don't like my choux pastry to be too dry. Experience will tell you when they are cooked to your liking.

# INDEX

## A

almond sponge pudding, baked,
    with coffee cream
    sauce   210–11
apple, ginger and mustard soup,
    chilled   141–2
apple and lemon tarts with bilberry
    sauce with gin   211–12
apple, sage and onion purée   132
apricot purée   181
apricot rum puddings, baked   202
Athol brose   184–5
avocado pear salad with yoghurt and
    capers   65
avocado, prawn and banana salad
    with salt pecan nuts and
    yoghurt dressing   74–5
avocado with redcurrant and orange
    dressing   72–3

## B

bacon sticks   113
beef, boiled fillet of and caper
    sauce   149–50
beetroot soup, chilled   27–8
blackcurrants, jellied fresh   189–90
blancmange   186–7
bread and butter pudding   200–1
broccoli omelette salad   77–8
broth, clear fish   24–5, 28; with
    seafood and fennel   28
broth, clear mushroom   26
burn't cream, English   178

burn't cream pancakes   214–15
burn't creams with ginger and
    raspberries   179–80
butter   11–12
    chive   109–10
    clarified orange   44–5
    mace   35
    orange chive   78–9
    tomato   107–8

## C

caramel pudding, steamed   209–10
carrot soup, cream of   32–3
carrot sticks, glazed, with ginger
    and orange   87–8
cauliflower cheese   86–7
celeriac, pan-braised   86
celeriac purée   91
cheese and shrimp fritters   59–60
cheesecakes, eighteenth-century
    almond   169–75
chicken
    aspic   50
    breasts of chicken with pecans and
        apples and Stilton sauce   122
    chicken, avocado and grapefruit
        salad with walnut
        dressing   76
    double chicken breasts stuffed
        with spinach, cottage cheese
        and nib almonds   116–17
    fricassee of chicken with
        vegetables   117–18

grilled spring chicken with
grapefruit, ginger, honey and
herbs 123–4
minced chicken with rice
118–19
pot-roast chicken breasts Nell
Gwynn with orange and
mushroom sauce 125–7
roast chicken with ham and
chestnut stuffing 121
roast chicken with Westphalia
ham, cracked wheat and celery
stuffing 119–20
roast stuffed double chicken
breast with glazed chestnuts,
bacon sticks and creamy bread
sauce 112–14
spiced breast of chicken with
whisky and pineapple 115
sausages 124–5
skewers with apple and
whisky 61–2
stock 22–4
chocolate sponge turnovers 182
'Christmas' salad with Red Windsor
dressing 75–6
Christmas soup 40
cock-a-leekie soup 41
coconut whisky roll 175–6
consommé
game 21
fish 24–5
courgettes 85–6
crab
elegant crab fish cakes on mini
muffins 106–8
Michael Smith's special crab
salad 80–1
potted crab with oranges 44–5
spiced crab-stuffed eggs 46–7
cranachan 184
cucumber, mint and buttermilk
salad 64
custard cream 177–8

## D

duck
pan-fried duck breasts 139
roast boned duck legs with
plums 135–9
warm duck salad 134–5
duckling, roast, with apple, sage and
onion purée 131–3

## E

eggs, scrambled, with
rosemary 49
eggs, spiced crab-stuffed 46–7
endive, baked, with pears and cream
cheese 89
endive, chicken-stuffed, with basil
and pistachio nuts 114–15
English winter salad with Red
Windsor dressing 75–6
Eton mess 169

## F

fennel 17
fish 93–110
fish pasty, rich 105–6
fricassee of fish in mustard
sauce 101–2
new fried fish 94

## G

green bean, bacon and rice salad,
hot 79–80

## H

haddock fish cakes with enriched
tartare sauce 95–6
halibut, pan-fried, with red peppers,
ginger and orange 96–7

ham, chicken and 'Brie' pasty, glazed, with watercress 162–3
ham and chicken creams wrapped in lettuce leaves with scallion sauce 161–2
ham and chicken mousse 51–3
herb garden salad 71
herb garden soup, chilled 30–1
herbs 16–18

## I

Iceberg lettuce with Stilton dressing 66
ices 192–8
  apple and rose petal cream ice 195
  blackcurrant purée 196–7
  brown bread ice-cream with rum 197–8
  coconut ice-cream with plum sauce 193–4
  custard ice-cream, basic 197–8
  lemon ice 193
  orange water ice 194
  raspberry cullis 196
  rhubarb ice 195–6
  stock syrup for water ices 192
  summer fruit salad ice 194–5
Irish stew 155

## J

jellied fresh blackcurrants 189–90
jellied orange fillets 188–9
jelly, white wine 109–10

## K

kidneys, creamed, with apples 163

## L

lamb

curried lamb with apple and pineapple 156
fillet of lamb reform 151–3
roast fillet (or boned loin) of lamb with leek sauce 150–1
Lancashire hot pots 157
leeks, creamed, with garlic and chives 85
leek and grape salad 64–5
lemon and grape jelly 192
lemon tarts 176–7
liver, calves', with pink grapefruit 164
liver, calves', with sherry vinegar, onions and mushrooms 164–5
'London Particular' (rich pea soup) 36–7

## M

meat 141–66
meringue topping 201–2
mousses
  chocolate, with coffee sauce 183
  England's four smoked fish 56–7
  ham and chicken 51–3
  triple pepper 49–51
  watercress 60
muffins, mini 107
mulligatawny 39
mushroom, tomato, orange and walnut soup 37–8
mussel soup, cream of, with saffron 32

## O

omelettes
  red pepper omelettes stuffed with turkey in horseradish cream sauce 140
  savoury rolled omelette stuffed with cottage cheese and shrimps 55–6

orange
    jellied orange fillets   188–9
    orange, avocado and smoked
        salmon salad   78–9
    orange, red onion and walnut
        salad   81–2
oxtail soup with chestnuts   38–9
oysters, baked, with cream and
        Parmesan   100–1

## P

pancakes   213
    burn't cream pancakes   214–15
    whisky buttercream
        pancakes   213–14
partridge, butter roast, with Madeira
        cream sauce   128–9
pasta with cream and lemon   61
pastry
    choux   217–18
    flaky   215–17
    rich shortcrust   217
pears in sweet white wine with
        candied lemon spirals   190–1
pear tarts   212
pheasant, roast, with ginger and
        orange   127–8
pineapple, melon and pear
        salad   191–2
plum puddings   205–6
pompion soup   40
pork
    pork fillet with mustard and
        apples   158
    roast boned loin of pork with
        tomato Madeira gravy   159–60
    sugared spiced pork chops with
        apple and walnuts   160
potato and apple salad   66–71
potato cream soup   29–30
potato and mushroom
        ramekins   89–90
potatoes, mashed   91–2

poultry and game   111–40
puddings,
    baked almond sponge pudding
        with coffee cream
        sauce   210–211
    baked apricot rum puddings   202
    baked walnut orange
        pudding   204–5
    bread and butter pudding   200–1
    plum puddings   205–6
    redcurrant and hazelnut roly-poly
        pudding   203–4
    steamed caramel
        pudding   209–210
    summer pudding   187
purées   90–2

## Q

quail, warm salad of   130–1
quails' eggs, tartlet of, with cottage
        cheese and smoked
        salmon   47–8
queen's puddings   201–2

## R

ratafia trifle   180–1
redcurrant and hazelnut roly-poly
        pudding   203–4
rice, savoury   88
rice pudding, rich   168
rum custards   179

## S

salads   63–82
salmon
    light salmon kedgeree   108–9
    poached salmon with sherry
        cream sauce   99–100
    potted salmon, marbled with
        turbot and scallops   54–5

potted salmon and turkey with
    honey-mint sauce  58–9
ragout of salmon, scallops and
    prawns in white wine
    sauce  102–5
smoked salmon 'scones'  45–6
smoked salmon soup, chilled,
    with smoked trout  29
spinach and salmon
    'custard'  53–4
sauces
    apricot  185–6
    bilberry  211–12
    blackcurrant and liquorice  154
    bread, with cream  124–5
    caper  149–50
    caramel  209
    coffee  183
    coffee cream  210–11
    cranberry  98
    cream  206
    honey-cream  203
    honey-mint  58–9
    honey-walnut  204–5
    leek  150–1
    Madeira cream  128–9
    mustard  101
    mustard and caper  146
    orange hazelnut  133–4
    orange and mushroom  126–7
    plum  136–9, 193–4
    redcurrant  203
    reform  152–3
    scallion  161–2
    sherry cream  100
    tartare  95–6
savoy cabbage with caraway  84
semolina puddings, chilled  185–6
shellfish with quails' eggs in white
    wine jelly  109–10
shepherd's pies, mini  144–5
sole, Dover, fillets of, with prawns,
    radicchio and martini
    sauce  97–8

soups  19–42
    chilled apple, ginger and
        mustard  41–2
    chilled beetroot  27–8
    chilled herb garden  30–1
    chilled smoked salmon with
        smoked trout  29
    chilled spinach and
        watercress  35
    Christmas  40
    clear  21–2
    cock-a-leekie  41
    cream of carrot  32–3
    cream of mussel with saffron  32
    cream of vegetable, rich  31
    creamy white turnip  27–8
    'London Particular' (rich
        pea)  36–7
    mulligatawny  39
    mushroom, tomato, orange and
        walnut  37–8
    oxtail with chestnuts  38–9
    pompion  40
    potato cream  29–30
    tomato and plum  25
    turnip  27–8
    walnut  37–8
spinach and salmon 'custard'  53–4
spinach and watercress soup  35
spinach, wilted, with lemon,
    nutmeg and garlic  84
sponge puddings, mini  215
starters  43–62
steak
    pan-fried fillet steak with mustard
        and caper sauce  145–6
    steak, kidney and mushroom
        pies  142–3
    steak, kidney and mushroom
        pudding  147–8
stock  15–16, 20–5
    beef, basic rich brown  20–1
    chicken  22–4, 50
    clear  21–2

fish, strong   24–5
  game, rich   21
stuffing   112–13, 119–20
sugars   13
summer pudding   187
syllabub   181


## T

tomato and plum soup   25
tomato and red onion salad   73
triple cream pudding   177–8
triple pepper mousse   49–51
trout
  fillets of rainbow trout with
    cranberry sauce   98
  pan-fried trout with two
    herbs   99
  potted smoked trout with
    horseradish   48
  smoked   29
turkey scallops, butter-fried,   133–4

turkey, fricassee of, with smoked eel
    and soured apples   129–30
turnip soup, creamy white   27


## V

veal, pan-fried, with sage leaves,
    apricots and cream   165–6
vegetables   83–92
venison, braised, with blackcurrants
    and liquorice   153–4


## W

walnut oil dressing   76
walnut orange pudding   204–5
watercress mousses   60
whisky buttercream
    pancakes   213–14


## Y

Yorkshire mince plait with pickled
    walnuts   143–4